the a
unruly
travel
on a
budget

MW00620756

calen ann otto

a guide to traveling the USA on a
small budget as ethically &
creatively as possible

THE ART OF UNRULY TRAVEL ON A BUDGET
Copyright © 2021 by CALEN ANN OTTO

ISBN: 978-0-578-96236-8

All rights reserved. No part of this publication may be reproduced, distributed, or transmitted in any form or by any means, including photocopying, recording, or other electronic or mechanical methods, without the prior written permission of the publisher or author, except in the case of brief quotations embodied in critical reviews and certain other noncommercial uses permitted by copyright law.

Although every precaution has been taken to verify the accuracy of the information contained herein, the author and publisher assume no responsibility for any errors or omissions. No liability is assumed for damages that may result from the use of information contained within.

—105—
PUBLISHING
EST. 2020

WHAT READERS ARE SAYING ABOUT *THE ART OF UNRULY TRAVEL ON A BUDGET*

"Of all the travel guides I've looked at this is the only one I have ever read from cover to cover and was sad to see it end. This guide is full of fascinating true stories, tips I hadn't thought of before, and gorgeous photos, as well as many helpful hints and resources. I am inspired to travel, meet new friends, and see the beautiful U.S. on a budget after reading. This book is brilliantly written from the heart. I will definitely follow the author's blog and will be looking forward to the next book."
– Kim Beller, artist, activist, and creator of the Art Nest Podcast

"The Art of Unruly Travel on a Budget is a perfect guide for travelers of all ages looking to explore the United States and looking for some help doing it! Calen provides an insightful and detailed guide into travelling the USA on a tight budget, while taking into account the ethics of tourism along with the challenges and risks of travelling alone. From plant-based eating to safety tips, the guide provides practical information with a wonderful personal feel."
- Abdourahamane Ly, climate, racial, and animal rights activist

"There's nothing stopping you from traveling around the US...even with no or little money! You don't have to be afraid to explore with the tips and helpful advice you'll receive from Unruly Travel. Calen breaks down all the ways you can travel cheaply, how to make money on the road, where to stay on a dime, and more. This book is packed with ideas you may not have thought of and resources to help you travel on the cheap."
- Christy Morgan, author of *Blissful Bites*

"Lots of guidebooks claim to be great resources for budget travel, but they rarely go beyond listing hostels and cheap hotels and telling you how to get discounts with a student card. This book is different. If you have a sense of adventure and a desire to explore the USA, Calen Otto will show you how you can make your dream a reality, no matter how small your budget is. They speak from experience, as they traveled across the country for months with nothing but a $300 gift card when they started their journey. If you follow the tips and suggestions in this book, not only will you make your money stretch farther, you will also have many unexpected adventures and make unexpected connections with people along the way, which are sure to be your most lasting memories of your trip."
- Wendy Werneth, founder of The Nomadic Vegan

Unruly Travel

Where do I begin?

I've never put so much energy into concentrating my knowledge on one subject before. I've never thought I would understand something so deeply that my advice on the subject would be undeniably meaningful. But look where we are now! I am ready to offer ideas, instructions, stories, information, budget tips, and travel magic based on my own experiences as an unruly traveler. Are you ready to roll?

This book is dedicated to all the earth cookies who are following their moral compass and paving new paths, regardless of the growing pains.
To all the unruly wanderers.

This book would not have made it into your hands without the time, effort, and brilliance of a few special folks: Helen Otto, Charlie Sudlow-Maestas, Kim Beller, Christy Morgan, Tim Burdine, Patricia Jones and JL Raynor from 105 Publishing, and others. The support and love from Casey Otto, Ellen Selm, Meg Taiclet, Kasyn and Wesley Kile, Rivers Wilder Green, and Anne Beukel Bak is invaluable to me. Thank you Daniel Turbert, Mo Seyam, Ben Gromley, and Sara Engblom for being my trusty travel partners over the years.

Travel Magic

"We are travelers on a
cosmic journey, stardust, swirling
and dancing in the eddies and whirlpools of infinity.
Life is eternal. We have stopped for a moment
to encounter each other, to meet, to love, to share.
This is a precious moment. It is a little parenthesis in eternity."

- Paulo Coelho, The Alchemist

Let's Begin!

I personally know and understand that travel can be intimidating at times, but with this guide, we'll try to make it a little less challenging and more enjoyable. **The purpose of this guide is to help you learn how to travel the USA (United States of America) on an *extremely small* budget by alternative travel methods. I'm talking about walking out of your house to adventure and move about with only a few hundred dollars or less!**

I've crossed the USA a handful of times—two of those times starting with hardly any cash in my pocket, working as I went. My second trip was much easier because I had already figured out how to get around the USA with little money. Throughout my process of beginning, attempting, failing, succeeding (whatever that means?), and making it up as I go, I've evolved into a confident and skilled traveler! With that being said, I'm here to share all of my knowledge with you so you can do the same.

First Things First

I want to acknowledge I am a white person, who lives in the USA, who many assume to be a woman and straight, even though I am non-binary and queer. This allows me to walk through the world with a lot of privilege that is not afforded to many others. So, what does that mean for this book? It means that I'm writing this from my point of view while trying my best to be mindful of how other people who have different experiences with privilege and marginalization participate in (or encounter) the same situations. Always follow your intuition and put yourself first!

How To Use This Book

I recommend using this guide in two different ways. One, consider reading it front to back—cover to cover— to wrap your brain around the alternative modes of travel I share with you. Some of these sections get a little technical, so skim when needed. Read the "Food for the Brain" sections for my personal stories corresponding to the topic at hand. I consider these the hidden gems of the book!

For option number two, I suggest carrying this book with you as a guide during and before travels so that you can pull it out when needed. From there it'll give you ideas and advice to help you keep on keepin' on. There is a list of hotlines in the back of the book for when times get hard and you need support.

A Note on Mantras

All of the mantras shared in this book were my personal mantras while crossing the USA by myself. Mantras aren't always statements that are already true. They are something that we hope for, wish for, and aspire to make real. They are to ground and calm you. Use my mantras, switch them up, or come up with your own!

My Last Note, Before You Begin

It'll be easier to understand my travel methods if you consider that I'm offering you ways of budget traveling you don't always hear about. In fact, you may have never considered any of them. My advice to you: Be open to new ideas! Not all of these ways of travel will be your first inclination, and that's okay. The information is here for you to play with—take what you need and leave the rest. This book was created for people who are curious about unruly budget travel, are ready to hit the road, need some tips or support, and for those who just love a good travel tale.

"Making a decision
was only the beginning of things.
When someone makes a decision,
he is really diving into a strong
current that will carry him
to places he had never dreamed of
when he first made the decision."

- Paulo Coelho

1

Setting Intentions
and
Crafting Your Experience

"Man does not simply exist
but always decides
what his existence will be,
what he will become
in the next moment."

- Viktor Frankl

Before we get into the how-to, we must understand the why or why not?

Knowing *why* you're choosing to adventure somewhere is even more important than knowing *how*, or your destination. The why will help you craft how to start, organize modes of transportation, set intentions along the way, and target destinations. The beauty of setting intentions and spending conscious moments with this question of "why travel?" is that you honestly may not know, and that's completely okay as well. If this is you right now, I suggest asking yourself what types of feelings you're looking for through travel, instead of specific reasons.

Before we pull out the boots and backpack, let's tackle some important questions:

1. **Are you feeling inspired to travel? If so, what led you here?**

2. **What specific *feelings* are you hoping to find during your travels?** *This can be anything such as free, lost, excited, welcomed, scared, or surprised.*

3. **What are ideas or things are you looking to find specifically through your travels?** *This can be anything such as your passion in life, new friends, a new species of plant, or a long-lost sibling.*

4. **What comfort levels are you desiring throughout this trip?** *You may be looking for anything from a simple patch of dirt to sleep on each night to five-star hotels that have hot tubs in each room. (If you picked a five-star hotel, this may not be the guide for you!)*

5. **Are you planning to travel with someone? How much alone time are you looking for? *(Or: How can you manage that need while physically with/near someone?)***

6. **How much time are you allowing yourself to travel?**

7. **What are your biggest fears around travel and this specific trip?**

I advise finding some time and a quiet space where you can fully answer these questions. Consider writing them down and dating them for a future reference point.

If I would have filled out this questionnaire before my first trip across the USA, it would have looked like this:

1. Yes, I am feeling inspired to travel. I'm not quite sure exactly how I got here—but it hasn't been the most fun. I'm feeling super down and ready for some fresh sights. I want to know that good still exists in the world, and that I can push myself to do things that scare me, *while* still trusting myself.

2. Hmm. Feelings. I am looking for feelings of just plain fun; I'm looking to feel happy, whole, connected, and new. I've been feeling too much "blah" lately.

3. I only know a couple of specific things I am looking to find through this trip. One, I want to learn how to bike tour + ride my bike across the United States. Two, I am looking for new faces + places that I haven't been to before. I don't really have any big plans, but I do know that I am looking to be inspired and hopefully surprised by the compassion of the world.

4. I don't have any high requirements for comfort throughout this trip. I am planning on taking my tent, not showering consistently, and making it up as I go. So, I don't expect to be super comfortable most of the time. Let's see how comfortable I can feel without my everyday items and rituals.

5. I am planning on traveling solo. I am looking for a lot of alone and quiet time, specifically time in nature. I am not opposed to traveling with someone else if the opportunity arises and it feels right.

6. I don't have a set timeline for this trip. I intend to take the time that I need, but hopefully, be gone no more than four months or so. Who knows, I may just move to California when I get there!

7. I have a few big fears around this trip. I have never traveled with such little money before, so I'm not sure if it's going to work. I am more specifically worried about people not allowing me to work for food if I don't have a lot saved up. I'm also a little scared that people may try to take advantage of me. And oh, I am scared about bike touring. I've never done it before, and honestly, I don't understand what I'm reading about bikes.

As you can see, this process of asking ourselves questions and examining our thoughts helps us to set intentions and give some pre-direction to our travels. Even if you don't understand what you're doing or how you're going to do it, that's okay. The fact that you're even starting is incredible.

Safety tips for emotional health throughout this process:
- If you don't know, don't stress! If you feel like you need to come up with answers, but they just aren't happening, return to this at another time.
- Don't shove yourself into a box. Dream big and let your imagination play. Avoid denying yourself what your spirit is truly asking for while dreaming, even if it seems out of reach!

Mantras:
- I easily mold and craft my experience at every moment.
- I don't shrink my desires to please the general society; the world is evolving to learn how to care and embrace me.

Resources:
- ***The Alchemist***: This is a book by Paulo Coelho. In a more creative and story-like way, Paulo shows us how our energy affects our lives, what creative energies we carry inside of us, and how to ignite our inner lights. I recommend reading this before or during travels!

2

Before You Hit the Road, Jack

"A ship in harbor is safe —
but that is not what ships are built for."

- John A. Shedd

Preparing To Leave

Before you get to the candy and sweetness of this guide, we have to do a little housecleaning together. There are a few things that you may want to do to feel a little more prepared, confident, and ready to go. As always, you have the choice to skip this part, but these activities and questions have given me a security blanket during extended travels. During our last exercise together, you may have found a bit of direction for your travels. Now, let's start making some real plans. The answers to those questions will directly affect how much, or little, you feel that you need to do here. In this section, we'll learn how to pull together extra cash, leave spaces feeling settled, and find your breathing lighthouse.

Pulling Together Cash

But *wait*...Isn't this guide supposed to tell you how to travel with very little money? Yes! Indeed. You can take the no money route, but if it's your first time traveling on a very small budget, you may feel safer with some emergency cash or a little bit to get you started. If you don't have a consistent job to put away a little into savings, here are three big ways to acquire that dough, with different suggestions for each one.

1. ## Ask your friends, family, community, or random wealthy people!

   There is nothing wrong with asking for help, and those who surround you might be excited at the opportunity to help you reach for your dreams and travel goals.

   a) ### Create A GoFundMe
   For my first trip across the USA, I started a GoFundMe and came up with $1,175 from people who wanted to support me and be a part of my bike trip. It was enough cash to buy a new bike and some used supplies. **There's no shame in asking for help and support from your community. In an ideal world we would all have time to rest, heal, play, have**

fun, explore, travel, and receive community support. There could be very privileged and wealthy people around you that are willing to share money with you for your travel projects, trips, and goals.

Simply go to **gofundme.com** and create an account with your Facebook account or email. After you're logged in, find "Start a campaign." You'll then be asked for your goal amount, title, and who you're raising money for. This doesn't have to be tricky— if you have an idea of your monetary needs already, that's a perfect place to start. If not, come back to this portion of the guide after you've seen my **suggested items list under "What to Bring"**, and figured out your needs a little bit more.

After you enter the mechanical details of your zip code and category of this project, you'll be prompted to upload a photo or video. I highly suggest that you don't skip this step—people love to see the face or the idea that they're supporting.

And now, fellow earthlings, we need your storytelling skills. The website will now prompt you to tell your own story. *Who are you? What are you asking for? Why are you asking for it? How can people directly help you? Why should they? Is there anything in it for them?* These are all questions that can help you craft your story. Be forward and real. Don't stress! You can always come back and edit this part of your campaign at any time.

Hot Tip: Include your supporters throughout your process if you want to do so! How can you let them in on your journey? I find that a simple way to keep them involved is to promise updates. This doesn't have to be anything major. Try a once-a-month check-in with a couple of pictures to help supporters stay engaged and feel a part of something big. You can even start a blog to document your journey through photos, videos, and stories for them to follow!

After you're all set up it's time to share, share, and share some more. The website will walk you through ways that you can share your campaign, so take advantage of this. Remember, *they don't know if they don't know*. You have to keep posting, asking, and reminding people that you would appreciate their help on your adventure.

Once you've received some cash and are ready to take it out, hit "withdraw." You'll have to connect a bank account and go through some security measures to make sure that you're really the person behind the account. This step is pretty easy. With the help of the website, your money will be deposited into your account in no time.

b) Literally, Ask

I've noticed that in today's society it is harder for us to ask for what we need. It may stem from a place of not feeling worthy enough, not wanting to inconvenience others, or just the anxiety of asking. **One of the many corrupt values that are drilled into our heads in the USA is that we must "pull ourselves up from our bootstraps" and weather the storm alone! Capitalism has also instilled deep in our bones the idea that we need to be productive at all times, working to be worthy of anything. That getting anything handed to us is a shameful thing. I disagree.**

Does grandma like to give you $36.00 each Christmas? Was Uncle Marty planning on giving you some cash for a graduation gift? Do you know some wealthy people who have nothing better to do with their money? Do you have loving friends who support your dreams and love seeing you living your best life?

Reach out to them if you have those people in your life. Please remember: People are allowed to say "no." And if they do, you didn't fail. You are asking a *question*, and that makes it open to all different types of responses.

You can call them on the phone, post a status on Facebook, shoot them a text message, ask face to face, or send a smoke signal. You never know—most likely some people in your life want and are willing to help out, and all you had to do was ask.

Expressing gratitude in a way that feels sincere to you is always appreciated. I'm a big fan of handwritten "Thank You" notes and snail mail. It's always an unexpected delight to receive appreciation in the mailbox.

I also want to acknowledge some folks do not have supportive family or community members to reach out to and ask for money. Some do but those people do not have extra money to give to be spent on travel and other things that are not necessities. This is a real situation for many people. Let's think of some more ways to make some cash!

2. Start Selling Stuff

A good portion of us have too much junk. Right? Take a look around. What can you get rid of? Clothes? Shoes? Your parents' electronics? Books? A car? Your iPad? Cousin Jimmy's CDs? Just as we learned by watching *Frozen*, let it go.

a) Selling Online

This seems to be the most popular way to sell/buy used items in today's world. There are a few different places where you can post your items.

Try Facebook

On your own personal page, create a new post. Upload a clear picture of the item that you're selling, a small but detailed description of the item, and your asking price. Sit back, and (hopefully) watch the comments roll in. One person's trash is another person's treasure, right? (Yes, I did edit this to be non-gendered.)

Use Facebook Yard Sales

It's kind of strange but super helpful. The humans of Facebook have created different Yard Sale groups, in which you basically set up a virtual yard sale anywhere in the USA. In your Facebook search bar, just type in your city's name and "yard sales." There should be groups around you that will pop up. In many places, there are multiple groups.

Be careful. Remember, you're still on the internet interacting with the humans of this planet. Don't publicly give out personal information to strangers.

Once you've joined your local yard sale group, you can start posting your items. You'll create posts the same way that you would post them on your personal Facebook, so refer back to the **first** paragraph above for instructions.

If someone decides to buy your item, you'll receive a comment on your post or a personal message from them. From there, you can discuss the details, location, and time of your transaction.

You have a couple of options: Exchanging through the mail or in person. If you decide to exchange in person, stay safe by doing it in a public place and taking a buddy with you. The good thing about in-person transactions is you can get cash for your item, and the deed is done.

If you decide to exchange your item for cash through the mail, make sure that they pay you at least half of the requested price first, and communicate specific details. Once the buyer is ready to pay, you'll have to agree on a method. My favorite online place of transaction is **PayPal,** but many other apps allow you to send money to strangers quickly.

A note about scams: If you are selling anything, be very mindful of people paying for items via PayPal and other money exchange apps. Some people craft scams where you receive a realistic-looking email "confirmation" that you have received money, but in fact, you haven't received anything. Many people lose their valuable items this way, having sent the item without actually receiving any money, and it often can't be retrieved. The only way to be certain that you've got money is to check your balance on the PayPal website, or other services, themselves!

Use Apps
If you have a smartphone, you can try selling your items through different apps. I say "try" because sometimes this can seem like a slow process. Some popular apps for selling clothing are thredUP, Letgo, VarageSale, 5miles, Poshmark, Depop, and Wallapop.

Some apps for selling other items outside of clothes are Carousell, Boxes, SellSimple, and Shpock. There are thousands of different apps out there, so play around and find the ones that suit you best.

Use Craigslist or eBay
Although they are set up differently, they both share a similar idea. You post your items, create a description, and share it with a world of thirsty consumers. On Craigslist, you'll be posting specifically to your zip code area, so you'll probably have more local interaction. On eBay, you're selling to a wider audience, so there might be some shipping involved. Both sites ask for an item name, description, and picture. It'll be a similar process to the one I explained for posting your items for sale on your own personal Facebook.

If you use eBay, you'll have to create an account and link some sort of card and bank account. eBay even has an app that makes the set-up and selling process pretty easy. If you use Craigslist, you have a lot more freedom to choose how you wish to handle your transaction. Again, be on the lookout for scamming emails.

Always keep safety in mind and don't go through with a deal if you don't feel right or comfortable about the interaction. You can decide not to sell to someone at any time, even if they're already at your planned meeting place. Meet during daylight hours in public places. Be sure to let someone know where you are going and how long you will be gone! Your safety is worth more than anything. There will always be someone else in the world who wants to buy your items.

3. Share Your Talents or Services

What do you excel at doing in your life? What do you have to offer to the world? Maybe you're a yoga teacher, give great foot massages, know how to garden and want to teach others, or can belt out some tunes. How can you get paid for your talents and services?

a) Offer a Service

Listen, it's a weird world out there. People have all sorts of needs. Chances are you can fill one or two of them. Let people know what you are capable of, and that you're looking for some compensation.

What can you teach to someone? This is a great question to start with. If you excel in a subject, consider tutoring someone who wants to learn. If you know how to work with social media, or as an online accountant, start searching for some clients. Are you catching my drift?

Hot Tip: Even if you're not "qualified" to do something on paper or by some sort of degree, it doesn't mean that what you know isn't valid or of great service to someone else. Consider offering some references from people you have worked with before.

b) Offer Yourself Up for Odd Jobs

If you're on a time crunch, this could be something perfect for you. Start letting people know you are available to help them with odd jobs, and willing to learn new skills, if necessary.

You never know what needs people have. Your old boss might need someone to help organize their closet, your best friend needs someone to paint their walls magenta, or your neighbor needs someone to let Humphrey the dog out every two hours. Put it out there and rise to the occasion.

As you can see, there are multiple different ways to come up with some extra cash. The good news is that there are so many more ways than what is mentioned here, so let your imagination run wild. Many of these suggestions may seem like "lemonade stand" ways to make money, but when it comes down to it and you're on the road, you might be grateful for those lemons.

Take it from Me

I couldn't close this section without mentioning some of the things I've done for travel money. The first one that might be surprising to people is when I sold my hair for $500.00 on the internet. Yep, you read that right! I had been growing it out for almost my entire life, only chopping it dramatically a couple of times before I traveled to Thailand in 2019. Money wasn't my motivation to shave my head. I didn't even know that there was a big market for human hair. I shaved it to get to know myself better (underneath aesthetic layers), find out more about my gender, and because Thailand is downright freaking hot. Who knew I would get so much out of the experience!

When I lived on the east coast, I would often go traveling for four to six months, come back and work, only to start all over again when the travel bug bit. During those months at home, it was hard to keep a steady job because I was all over the place. My friend knew this and recommended that I try life modeling. He thought it may come easy to me because of my yoga asana practice. Low and behold, he was right!

I started modeling at an art museum, 100% naked, for $20.00 an hour in three-hour sessions. It was a great way to make money while meditating and getting more comfortable in my own skin.

Check out the video of me getting my head shaved in Thailand in the resources below. The video is included in the article titled "Why We Turned on the Clippers and Didn't Stop Until Our Hair Was Gone." I along with two other incredible queer people wrote sharing the motivations behind getting a buzzcut.

Leaving Spaces Feeling Settled

When I left home for my first tour across the USA, it was pretty easy because I was living with my parents. That meant I didn't have to find someone to take over a lease, get out of a contract, or pack up my room. The second time that I left was a different story.

What is your living situation like?

Before leaving, you'll want to feel settled and complete in leaving your current living situation, so you don't have things to worry about while you're on the road. You know the drill: we have to start asking some questions. Are you coming back to the space that you're currently in? If so, do you know when? Are you ever planning to come back? Do you need to store items somewhere safe or move them? Do you have other animal companions that will need to be cared for? I can't make these decisions for you or even guide you to find the answers. This will be something that you do on your own. Sorry, champ.

Whatever your answers are, even if they're unknown, start making plans to get everything situated as soon as possible. Ask people you know to help with these arrangements instead of paying expensive companies. If you can leave with peace of mind, you'll be able to handle difficult situations with more ease as they arise during your time on the road.

Find Your Breathing Lighthouse

Up until now, everything that we've discussed in this chapter has involved physical activities for you to check off your list. Now, let's take a break and hop into the emotional and spiritual side of things.

As I've learned through years of travel, it isn't always smooth sailing. No matter what the forecast says, we can't always predict storms, and we don't always have our raincoats. To help weather the storm, find your breathing lighthouse.

This can be any sort of animal: a human, cat, bird, Goddess, or your most trusted travel partner. I encourage you to find someone! Someone you know you can mentally and emotionally check in with when things get shaky. If you can't lock down a certain human person, consider finding a meaningful symbol or idea that can bring you peace and comfort in a moment of distress. This is your guiding light in the storm. This person, or practice, is there to help you meet your needs—finding healing, a laugh, direction, or solutions.

Who can you call when you've biked 40 miles and the last ten seem impossible? What can you do to find tranquility in yourself when plans fall through, and you don't know where you'll stay the night? For me, that's been my partners, best friends, parents, and yoga practice. I always know one of those people or my practice will be available when needed. I also know that most of the time I can find security within myself through my practice. Support systems, eh?

Safety tips for your physical and emotional safety while preparing to leave:

- Don't listen to the world if it tells you that you are not worthy enough of its time, energy, or monetary resources. Capitalism kills.
- When selling your items online, don't give out your location or any personal information. Have another human go with you if you decide to make an exchange in person.
- Be cautious on Craigslist. Some people aren't on there because they want to buy, sell, or trade items.

- Use discretion when choosing your "breathing lighthouse." Make sure that you find a force, within or outside of yourself, that can fiercely support, love, and provide care for you as needed from time to time.

Mantras:
- Everything I ask for is already finding me. The moment I asked for resources, the universe started sending them my way.
- I give my creative energies to the world and reap the benefits they sow.
- I always have a safe place to exist. The world is shifting around me to accommodate my needs.
- I am always loved, supported, and whole. I find sanctuary easily within others or myself.

Resources:
- **Guide to life modeling:** This will hopefully answer your questions about life modeling. *https://medium.com/swlh/how-to-be-a-great-life-model-41af79df46ea*
- ***Why I Shaved Off All of My Hair***: This article and full-length video will take you with me on a step-by-step journey into shaving my hair and liberating myself! You will also hear from two other brave souls as well. *http://wanderwoman.online/index.php/2020/11/07/goodbye-hair/*

3

How To Get Around

"Traveler, there is no path
the path is made by walking.
By walking you make a path
and turning, you look back
at a way you will never tread again."

— Antonio Machado

Modes of Transportation

I am completely stating the obvious here, but to get somewhere you actually have to go there. Let's look at some modes of transportation. I'll start the list with the ones I use the most, cost the least, and continue down the list in this fashion. We all have different abilities, so choose the ones that make the most sense to you.

In this chapter, I'll offer different modes of transportation—some more traditionally "comfortable" than the others. It's up to you to choose which one best meets your needs for each moment. In this section, we'll discuss ten main ways of getting around, along with different options and explanations for each mode of transportation.

1. Walking

Although I have never walked across the country, I know a couple of folks who have. The reason why walking made the top of the list is that it's free and gives you a fresh perspective on your surroundings.

Remember, all of these different options are exactly that—options. They can be started, ended, switched, swapped, and mixed. If you're considering walking as a main way of transportation, consider your desired route first. Are you hiking a trail? Walking on main roads?

Hiking

Hiking long trails can be dangerous, challenging, blissful, transforming, and rewarding. Although you are free to start any action at any time, I recommend seriously doing your research and planning if you're preparing to hike any trail. I'm not an expert on this topic (yet), but there are many other informational humans, guides, books, and websites to help you prep. I will share some with you in the resources section below.

If you're thinking about hiking a long trail, such as the Pacific Crest Trail (PCT) or the Appalachian Trail (AT), it will require a lot of research and preparation. This could fill up a whole other book, so make sure to begin your prep months in advance if you choose to hike a trail.

Walk Touring (As I Call it)

Now, let's talk about walking long distances. If you're considering walking a large number of miles, you may want to do a couple of things to prep.

- Map a route, or don't, but realize once you start walking, you'll need to know how far you are from food, water, and other necessities.

- Write out a list of factors to consider, and actually consider them: terrain, weather and seasons, road conditions, and elevation. Collect the gear you feel is needed for your specific walk and safety.

- Consider using a cart. Every human I've seen walking across the country so far has been pushing a cart to carry all of their gear and items. They seem to typically cost about $110.00. Where can you find one for free?

- Think about training. Do you feel you need to train? How little or how much? I'm personally not one to push training for activities like this too hard. But then again, I've never walked across the USA.

- When you're ready, put on your walking boots and let them do their thing! Speaking of boots, will you need an extra pair?

Food For the Brain

As someone who actually walked across the USA, Bryan Quocle shares:

"For one, the distance of a transcontinental walk at 2,500+ miles can be physically challenging. Whether you're pushing a cart or carrying a backpack, the strain and stress of continuous sojourns at 15 - 30 miles per day can quickly deplete your physical resources if you're not prepared. Weather and conditions can quickly wear you down, ranging from scorching heat to bitter snow, to high-velocity winds. The duration of the walk itself can push your emotional and spiritual limits. Most of the time, you'll be out by yourself in the scorching Southwestern deserts or endless fields of corn in the Midwest with little more to do than keep walking, anywhere from 4 to 12 months. I met a man who was walking from Maine down to Florida, across to California, then north into Washington; he'd been walking for more than 7 years coast to coast." (1)

For more information on longer trips, search *How to walk across the United States* on **Google**. There are tons of information and people breaking down exactly how it can be done. There's even a list started on Wiki of people who've walked across the USA, and it starts with my favorite: Mark Baumer. You can check out the list for yourself at the specified web address printed in the back of the book.

If you want some serious walking inspiration, check out Mark's blog, *Barefoot Across America* at **notgoingtomakeit.com.** Mark puts more poetic, raw, and sober energy into their work than we normally see in society. On day 100 of walking, Mark writes:

"An hour later two people in a white truck stopped and asked if I needed anything. I lied and said I didn't need anything instead of being honest and saying, 'I need you to admit climate change is real. I need you to do everything you can to fight for this earth. I need you to reject everything our fascist president tries to do to this world and its people.'" (2)

On a personal note, I love this travel blog more than any other one that I've ever read. While walking across the USA for the second time, Mark was hit by a car and died. Mark's work still lives on, and you can feel their spirit through everything that Mark has crafted. I highly suggest spending some time with Mark's work. Not only is Mark an inspiration for travelers, but humanity as a whole will benefit from taking notes from them. You can check out their blog, YouTube Vlog, or even buy their book *I am a Road* online.

> *"I need people to understand this earth does not only have to create systems of death and wealth."*

Although I could get lost in Mark's work, and the ideas of adventure, loss, and life as it exists, I'll let you do that on your own time.

"Tourist-Style" Walking

Yes, I made this word up, and yes, it's self-explanatory. While you're in new cities and towns, you may want to explore on foot if able. Although walking takes longer than using public transportation or calling an Uber, it's free. You may notice some things you wouldn't have if you weren't traveling as slow or close to the ground.

- Walking may give you the freedom to stop, go, run, jump, and play as you please. What can you notice along the way? I notice so many more details in nature, and tune into my surroundings more, when walking as opposed to driving or riding.

- If you have a smartphone, consider using **Google Maps** to help you get from place to place. As a side note, there is a section at the end of the book that lists all the apps that I have mentioned, and how to use them.

Other options are using a paper map, making a route up as you go, or asking humans for spoken and written directions. There's something very appealing and exciting about letting go of technology and doing it the old-fashioned way!

Food for the Brain

Some of my best memories I have locked in of big cities and small towns are the ones where I was taking on the new space by foot. During walking or running, I've gotten lost countless times and had to find a way to eventually feel confident in my direction again. If this is something you can do, I highly recommend it!

During my time at an animal rights conference one summer, a friend told me he had taken a bus to Berkeley where we were all meeting, but it didn't take him far enough into the city. His phone was dead, and he wasn't quite sure how to get there, so he just started walking and asking for directions. Sixteen miles later, he made it to the event, with a big ole smile on his face. Although that's not the way that everyone would have reacted to that situation, or felt about walking, it's an option that's sitting on the back shelf, just waiting for you to reach it.

Safety tips for walking long or short distances:
-   Make sure a human knows where you are leaving from and heading to. Check in frequently.

- Consider taking some form of self-defense class to get familiar with your body and how it can move.
- Consider buying a tracker and keeping it on you when it feels supportive.
- If you have an iPhone, consider turning on your location to be shared with someone.
- Make sure you know how far your next stop is; when you can get food, water, and any other supplies that you need.
- Bring proper gear to be protected from the elements.
- Stay hydrated and nourish your body with calories when needed.
- Be extra cautious when walking at night, especially alone. For femme, queer, trans, Black, Indigenous people, People of Color, and those embodying socially non-normative identities this is extremely important. It's sad but true, I try to avoid walking by myself anywhere after dark. We have to be extra cautious.

Mantras:
- My body safely and easily gets me where I need to go.
- I am conscious of every step I take, bringing me closer to my destination.
- My body is strong, protected, and easily supports me with every movement.

Resources:
- ***How To Walk Across All of The States*:** This resource is an interview from my podcast that gives you information, suggestions, and stories from a human who walked across the USA. Taylor Lancaster Thompson will let you know what to bring, how to prepare, how to start, and what to expect. *https://soundcloud.com/unrulystories/walk-usa*
- **Mark Baumer's blog:** Mark is the person we discussed above, and their written blog, and vlog, offer priceless information. Blog: *https://notgoingtomakeit.com*
  Vlog: *https://www.youtube.com/user/everydayyeah*
- ***Wild*:** This is a book and movie by Cheryl Strayed. It takes readers through the experience and story of her personal experience hiking the PCT as a solo female.

- ***#27 My Worst Days on The Trail Blew Away My Best Days Off | 2,650 Miles Of The PCT***: This is another podcast episode with Taylor, the same person who walked across the USA. This time he takes on the Pacific Crest Trail. From the technical side of gearing up for a huge hike to the nitty-gritty stories of trail magic, his episode is ideal for anyone interested in hiking the PCT, nature adventure, alternative living, and genuine human connection.
  https://soundcloud.com/unrulystories/taylor-pct

"For my part,
I travel not to go anywhere,
but to go. I travel for travel's sake.
The great affair is to move."

-Robert Louis Stevenson

2. Cycling

Unlike the last section of "Walk Touring" we just explored, I can now personally give you advice from my blood, sweat, crashes, and tears for this section. What is one way that you can cross the country virtually free (after possibly minimal upfront payments), while saving the environment some hurt, and pushing your body to its limits? Yep, you guessed it. Moving by bike.

If you're considering bike touring for your main mode of transportation, remember you'll have to start with a bike you're okay with riding each day. It doesn't have to be fancy, just something that works for you. If you take a look at guided bike tours, or even experienced cyclists, you may notice they all have some pretty expensive gear. Bikes can cost a pretty penny, and many folks will encourage you to get a specific touring bike. But I want to offer you some other options in this section... because that's how I roll.

When I began planning for my bike tour I didn't have a bike that would hold up crossing the country. So, I started a GoFundMe to pay for my bike. People were excited that they could help me with my dreams and goals, and I promised to update them along my trip. That's how I bought my bike.

The bike I ended up with was a road bike that cost $700.00 and wasn't meant for bike touring. But, at the time, it was the best one that fit my budget. After that, I also had to buy some gear, which cost another few hundred dollars.

You can either buy a bike and gear or ask around. There may be someone in your life who has some of the items that you need and are willing to give them to you. You also have the option of coming up with money by all of the means that we discussed in **chapter two** or using money that you already have.

When searching for bikes and gear, check out **Craigslist, eBay**, and bike groups on **Facebook**. In these spaces, you'll find mostly used items, that can be exactly what you need, for cheaper prices. I've also come across a handful of rad bike shops across the USA that will help you build your bike for free with used parts that are donated to them. Do some creative thinking, look around, and see what you can find. In the resources below you will be able to find directories of local bike shops across the USA!

Ask The Experts

When going through the process of finding a bike and gear, find local experts on the subject. Start with your local bike store! Go in simply to ask questions, pick their brains, and hear their advice. You never know, they may even be willing to donate a nice bike to you for the journey in exchange for giving them a shoutout!

Take everything with a grain of salt, though. When I was prepping for my bike tour, I went into a bike shop looking for some answers. I had my new bike with me—excited to get some gear and hear what they had to say. The person with whom I was working really got to me; they told me that I could never bike tour on the bike I had purchased, that it would break, and that it just wouldn't work. Five hundred miles, one crash, and only one popped tire later, my bike was still truckin' along.

My point is...listen to the experts and learn all you can from them but don't take every single word someone says as the absolute truth. Use your best judgment and seek out information from multiple sources. When looking for more information on bike touring, check out **Google**. It literally provided me with 80% of the information I needed.

How To Begin

The process of bike touring begins before you hit the road. You'll want to plan, even if it's just a little, on what direction you're headed, and what you need to take with you. A complete list of gear that you may want to take with you while biking across the USA can be found on

Rob Greenfield's website, which is included in the resources section below.

- Knowing where you may be headed is helpful; the terrain, climate, and general layout, will help you determine what sort of gear is needed.

The TransAmerica Trail

If you're looking to ride across the country, in some sort of "organized fashion," check out the **TransAmerica Trail**. It is a route that crosses the USA; either starting in Yorktown, Virginia, or Astoria, Oregon. You choose which way you ride the route. Keep in mind it isn't a bike trail, or even a special set of roads; the route takes you across the USA, on the same roads that are used for automobiles.

What's awesome about these maps is they are put together by **Adventure Cycling**, which can be found at **adventurecycling.org**. Let me tell you—they know their stuff. They also have complete sets of other maps that go all over the USA if you're not looking to bike on the TransAmerica Trail.

The maps provide you with everything you need to know including which roads to take, how many miles are in between each town or stop, what amenities are included in each town, and the specific details about climbs, hills, and drops in the road. They even include incredibly helpful resources on each map such as phone numbers and addresses to churches, parks, hostels, and other places where you can stay during your travels. I highly recommend these maps and am not sure I would have made it across the country without them.

- Once you have your route or direction in mind, make sure to gather everything you need. General items may include a bike, spare tires, extra spokes and other parts, gloves, a helmet, biking shorts, paniers, rain gear, GPS, water bottle(s), and other safety items.

- During this whole process, I suggest getting familiar with your bike and learning how it works. It will help you be more self-sufficient and make for an easier ride. When I was preparing for my trip, I watched a lot of videos on **YouTube.** From how to change tires and repair certain things on my bike, to the experiences that others had. YouTube is a great resource.

- Do you need to train during this time? How long and how much? This is a question you'll have to answer for yourself. It is helpful to physically train and do practice rides before you go, but not necessary.

- When you're feeling like it's time to hit the road, all you have to do is ride! It can seem intimidating to some folks but do your best to take it day by day and moment by moment.

Hot Tip: Later in this book, we will discuss how you can find places to stay. One big thing that we cover is **Couchsurfing**, which can be great to use during bike touring. For now, I have something even better to offer you. There is a special app, which is basically the same as Couchsurfing, but for cyclists. **Warm Showers** is a place where cyclists can offer up their home spaces for you to stay and help you out along your way. Hosts often offer their company, food, knowledge, and resources as well. For more information, check out **warmshowers.org**. Bonus: It's completely free!

Food for the Brain

Personally, I still have many mixed feelings about bike touring. When I started, I had no idea what I was doing. I had never attempted a single bike tour before and didn't understand what type of effort would be required to cross the country. Bike touring is simple and complex at the same time; it is simply moving pedals, which in turn moves a machine that takes your body wherever you direct the machine. On the other hand, you're doing constant work, climbing, coasting, descending, and learning along the way. You may have some tough days, and you may have to repair your bike every once in a while. You may be surprised to find there are so many resources, and people, to help you along the way.

As I mentioned, the first time I traveled across the USA, starting with $300.00 (which almost all went to bike repairs), was largely by bike. There were a lot of firsts for me; one, I had never crossed the country before. Two, I had never traveled on such a small budget before. And three, I had never bike toured before. With all things considered, I was pretty nervous, yet excited, at the same time. I was determined, yet scared, ready but hesitant but, as you do when you travel, I just did it.

After *WWOOF*-ing for a week in Virginia, I set off on my wheels. On the first day, I cycled about 67 miles. I had never biked more than 25 in my life. While I was panting underneath a tree in someone's yard on the side of the road, I realized the adventure may be more intense than I had thought. As time went on, I learned it was totally true. It was like I was learning how to walk again; I had to find my balance, stamina, and learn new skills.

Along the way, I met so many folks who were interested in what I was doing and wanted to support me. Some of them were familiar with cyclists because they were located along the TransAmerica Trail, and some had never heard of such a thing. Both groups of people amazed me. They opened up to me, invited me into their homes, and showed me love and care. Remember how I talked about hoping to meet compassionate people during my travels? Well, I found what I was looking for.

The hardest part of cycling for me was going down hills. On my second or third day of bike touring, I had gotten completely lost, and resorted to calling the police to pick me up (something which my privilege allowed me to feel safe doing – this may not be an option for many others, and I wouldn't do this now). I had gotten so far lost into the country on back roads even they had trouble finding me. When they did, they dropped me off on the side of the highway (where biking is usually illegal), leaving me with one choice of direction. When I got into some sort of commercial area, and off the dangerous highway, I felt completely worn down, and sat myself down at the corner of someone's yard.

At that moment I heard a sound coming from my phone... a notification from Tinder (yes, the infamous Tinder dating app). I decided to check it, because I really didn't know what else to do with myself, and later realized that it was the best decision I could have made at that moment.

A person from Tinder messaged me asking how my trip was going, if I needed help, and added that he had already biked the TransAmerica. I promptly responded "yes", and he was on his way to get me. I ended up staying with this person for about a week, and that was an adventure in itself. During that time, we ended up exploring and jumping through the river in Richmond, VA, climbing through abandoned buildings on the hunt for incredible views, and attending a wedding.

Even though I got off track from cycling in a very frustrating way, it turned out to be better than I had ever imagined. When it was time to go, my new friends dropped me back onto the trail. The experienced biker insisted I should climb the hill that we were parked below because it would offer the best views of the Blue Ridge Parkway.

And it did. It was spectacular! After climbing for hours, I crashed down the other side of the hill, smashed my bike, injured my back, and ended up with a mild concussion. Because of lack of preparation, I didn't know how to properly descend down hills... and that baby was a gnarly one. From then on, I let the fear of crashing stick with me, and it was an unforgettable undertone in every decision I made about cycling. Be sure to check out the podcast episode where I tell the story of my crash in full detail in the resources below!

If I could go back and change anything about that trip, I would work on my fear of falling. Although I wouldn't alter any experience I went through, I would try not to let fear drive many of my decisions. Cycling parts of the way across the country was one of the most challenging and exciting things I've ever done. I wanted to share these bits of a story with you so you can start to let your imagination run wild when planning for your bike tour. Although cycling will be a huge part of your travels if you decide to go this route, the people you'll experience along the way will make it all worth your while.

"Generally, I think that versatility is the most important aspect of being a vagabond traveler. Allowing yourself to bend to situations instead of the inverse allows me to see and do things from a different perspective. For example, I mainly travel by bicycle. It allows me to get the exercise I need, I can travel greater distances, and experience more natural settings. It also means that I can get out of dangerous situations more quickly than if I were backpacking or hitchhiking (both things I do regularly). At the same time, using a bike helps me not be so dependent on fossil fuels, money, etc. If I'm too tired to ride, I post up somewhere and enjoy a spot for a day. The added benefit of having a bike is that I can leave my stuff at a friend's or couch surfers, which gives me the opportunity to link up with some other cyclists and have some fun. Most times the simpler the better is the best way to go, but I love the flexibility that I have with bicycle travel."

– Taylor Lancaster Thompson

Safety tips for cycling:

- Start with a bike that feels right with your body and is suitable for long rides. Bring extra sets of tools and parts which might be needed.
- Learn how to work on your bike, so you are ready if and when it needs repairing.
- Do some sort of physical preparation to get your body used to riding long distances.
- Make sure you have enough water and calories to make it from stop to stop.
- Bring mace or something to protect yourself. Dogs love to chase cyclists. People can be creepy.
- Bring well-fitted gear that protects you during your ride and consider the climate when choosing gear.
- Let someone know your route and when you make it from place to place.
- If you do any riding at night (not suggested), make sure to have lights on your bike so you can see what's in front of you and so others can see you.
- Always wear bright clothes and a helmet while riding. Remember, not all drivers pay attention, or like sharing the road with bikers, so ride mindfully.

Mantras:
- My body is strong, safe, and supported.
- My bike works perfectly; working in sync with my body to get me where I need to go.
- With every new pedal forward, protective energy surrounds my bike.
- I always arrive at my desired destination safely.

Resources:
- ***My Gear for Cycling Across the USA***: This is Rob Greenfield's list for things to take with you when cycling across the USA. *http://robgreenfield.tv/cyclinggear/*

- **TransAmerica Trail information:** Here you can find the complete set of maps needed to bike the TransAmerica Trail. The website

also contains other information about maps, bike touring, and helpful resources.
https://www.adventurecycling.org/routes-and-maps/adventure-cycling-route-network/transamerica-trail/

- **When The Travel Bug Bites: My Unruly Travel History by Calen Otto**:
  Listen to podcast #2 of the series to hear about my epic and terrifying bike crash on the Blue Ridge Parkway.
  http://wanderwoman.online/index.php/2021/03/09/when-the-travel-bug-bites-my-unruly-travel-history-by-calen-otto/

- **100 Local Bike Shops in the USA by State**: This article will direct you to some awesome bike shops in the country.
  https://www.peacebicycles.com/advice/bike-shops-near-me#North%20Carolina

- **Local Bicycle Shop Directory:** Look up bike shops by state to find ones near you.
  https://www.bicycleshops.us

3. Ridesharing

Alright kiddos—it's time to unlearn half of the stuff our elders taught us growing up. And yes, I am about to encourage you to get into cars with strangers. At first glance, ridesharing can seem extremely scary, and in some cases it is. Before we jump into this section, it is important to note Indigenous women, Latinx women, Black women, disabled folks, and trans folks have a higher chance of being picked up and never seen again when compared to a white woman. An article by *The Missing* will be offered in the resources section of this chapter that explains "The Missing White Girl Syndrome." Not everyone is out there to hurt you; some people are genuinely interested in helping you along your way. Tailor this section to your own travels by taking what feels best and safest for you and leaving the rest.

Don't limit yourself to only finding rides online. Throughout my travels, I have found many necessary rides from point A to point B through word of mouth, meeting people that were headed in the direction that I wanted to go at the right moment or looking for rides on Craigslist. Always practice caution when connecting with people online.

So, what is ridesharing, exactly?

Ridesharing is simply the act of sharing a ride with someone else. Before we get into how to do it, please consider you never really know people, who they are, or their intentions, so you have to proceed with caution while traveling this way.

Word of Mouth

Have you ever told Dave you needed X object, and Dave told Sheila, and Sheila told their great grandparent Clover, and next thing you know, great grandparent Clover is digging through their attic, and you have desired X object sitting in your hand? Well, it doesn't always happen exactly like that, but ridesharing can work in similar ways.

- Where are you currently? Where are you trying to go? Do you already know someone headed that way? If so, consider asking to join them. You can possibly offer to help them drive, be another brain behind directions, or simply share your fabulous taste in music. You don't have to offer gas money, but if you have it and are willing to contribute in this way, people usually appreciate it.

- If you don't already know someone who is going where you are going, that's okay. Find them. Chances are that someone is headed in the same direction as you. If you don't believe me, look at the road that you're planning on traveling. Do you see people passing through? Start asking around. Ask the humans at the farm you're working at, at the hostel where you're staying, and at the grocery store where you're dumpster diving.

- Ask people to pass your general destination needs along. Someone might know someone that is already going your way, who could offer you a lift. Never tell people your exact location or address you are headed to!

Food for the Brain

During my bike tour across the USA, I decided I didn't want to force myself to pedal every single inch of the trail. If I had an interest in a different place than where I was, and didn't feel like biking, I would find rides—or they would find me. One day, I was staying at a church where I had spent the night. Although I am so far from religious in so many ways, and think that religion can be extremely harmful, I woke up and went to the service they had that morning. After the service, I was talking with some folks who were a part of the church. We started talking about my trip and I expressed my need to get to a certain city to the person that I was conversing with. They then called over their friend, who was headed in the same direction and leaving in thirty minutes.

Before I knew it, my bike was strapped to the roof of a five-seater car, and I was traveling a route to pick up kids for church camp with someone I had just met. It was actually quite interesting! I met three very different children and got to share my travel tales with them during my time in the car. Who knows...maybe one day they'll be giving you a ride!

Another time, I was trying to get from Los Angeles, California to Las Vegas, Nevada. I was working on a "farm" in the middle of the desert, and I didn't have much connection with the outside world. At the time, I didn't have a whole lot of cash on me, so taking a bus wasn't something I was considering.

The people working alongside me knew my desires, and one person helped me make them into a reality. My farm friend in Los Angeles had a friend from high school who was from Pennsylvania, living in Las Vegas, and visiting Los Angeles for the weekend. How perfect?! Not only because I am from the same area as them, but because I was looking to leave ASAP. Although I didn't know the person my friend had mentioned, I trusted his judgment, and gave him permission to reach out. Before I knew it, I was sitting in the car with a human named Patrick, riding through the desert, stopping to take photos at abandoned theme parks, sleeping on his couch, and making a (hopefully) life-long friendship. **Remember: Friends of friends are your rideshare friends.**

Meeting People "ATM"

Meeting people ATM, or "at the moment," isn't something I am able to directly teach you. Sometimes, you'll run into people who are able to help you out, without even trying. You could be sitting at a local bar drinking ginger ale or getting down in a community yoga class when you spark up a conversation with a stranger. If opportunities pop up during your everyday travel interactions, be open and willing to take them, as long as they feel safe.

Craigslist Rideshare

Although at first the thought of finding a ride off of the open internet made me cringe a little inside, due to the vastness of the internet, I'm happy to say that I've had all good experiences through Craigslist Rideshare. It's pretty easy to do as well! All you have to do is post where you need to go and when, wait for a reply, and then work out the details from there. For the cherry on top of deliciously dairy-free chocolate ice cream, it's free! For ideas on how to stay safe while in the car with strangers, check out my tips in the **"hitchhiking"** section of this chapter.

I'm confident when I say that you could make your way around the whole country using only rides from Craigslist. There's even a documentary about a human who decided to do this, called **Craigslist Joe**. So, let me tell you exactly how to catch some rides.

- Before you get onto Rideshare, you need to know where you're leaving from and some sense of where you're going. It's also helpful to have a time frame in mind.

- On the internet, go to **www.google.com**. From this search browser, you'll type in "Craigslist Rideshare" followed by the name of the city of your departure.

  For example, if I'm leaving from Chicago, Illinois, it would look like this:
  Search: Craigslist Rideshare Chicago

- Once you've found the Rideshare page attached to the place you're leaving from, you have a couple of options. One, you can search for the place you're going by searching the state name and city at the top of the page in the search bar. There may be trips people are taking that are already posted going to your destination. The second thing you can do, and I recommend, is posting your own request. To do this, find the "post" button at the right-hand corner of the top of the page.

- Once you've done that, the site will take you to a page with a few different options, asking you what type of post you're making. Select **"community."**

- Craigslist then asks you to choose a category. Select **"rideshare."**

- While continuing, Craigslist may ask you to choose a location which fits best, to get a more accurate idea of where you're leaving from. Select your desired location. Just because you've narrowed down a place doesn't mean your rideshare request will only show up to that small part of the city, it will still show up on the main site of the city as a whole.

- You'll then start filling out details about your needs.

1. **Posting Title:** This is where you'll type exactly what you're looking for. For this example, let's pretend like we're headed to Cleveland, Ohio.

   Your posting title will always be "Looking for a ride from **[city of departure]** to **[destination goal - if you know the city, enter that here]** on **[day of departure]**.

   If you have any details you would like to add, enter them after the day of departure. Some things to include may be:
   "Open to other dates"
   "Can offer gas money"
   "Willing to drive"
   "Has mind-blowing music to share"
   "Sensitive to smoke in cars"
   or even
   "Open to any destination"
   depending on how you're crafting your experience.

2. **Specific Location:** This is where you have the option to post an even more exact location of where you're leaving from. I usually skip this part, unless I am not going to be able to leave from another destination. For example, if I'm on the outskirts of Chicago and somehow couldn't find transportation downtown to meet up with a ride-sharer, I would post the specific place where I need to be picked up.

3. **Postal Code:** Enter the zip code of wherever you are. If you don't know it, ask someone around you or look it up on **Google**.

4. **Posting Body:** This is where you pull in the ride-sharers. Where are you headed, and when? What are you like? What do you have to offer?

   These are all questions you'll need to answer here. Give direct answers. Let's break them down a little bit more together.

   a) **Where are you headed, and when?** Tell humans who are offering rideshares where you are leaving from again, and where you are going. We're basically repeating the title in the first sentence of this question.

      It's also important to include when you are looking to head that way. If you have flexibility in your schedule, mention that as well. If you don't have a preference as to when, you guessed it: mention that.

   b) **What are you like?** I'm not asking you to give a full personality or body description here, or even disclose your age. I'm asking you to give the ride-sharers some insight as to who you are. Remember, they're letting you, a stranger, into their car, so they are going to want to know some personal details.

      Your sentence may look like this: I'm a traveler, in my **[age range]**, making my way to my next destination. I'm respectful, cool as hell, **[personal attribute]** and **[other description]**.

As for the spaces with the personal attributes and other descriptions, include two things about yourself that will hint to others what the car ride or exchange might be like. Are you easygoing? Let them know that you're just here to go with the flow. Are you super quiet? Let them know that there might not be much conversation during the ride.

posting title	city or neighborhood	postal code
RIDE NEEDED from Chicago, IL to Cleveland, C		22322

description

Hi,

I am a traveler, in my 20's, trying to make my way to my next destination. I'm open minded, easy going, and can offer gas money.

I am specifically trying to get from Chicago, IL to Cleveland, OH on October 13th. Please let me know if you are headed that way and we can work something out. Looking forward to hearing from you!

Thanks.

posting details

rideshare type

ride wanted

contact info

email

hellounrulytravel@gmail.cor

email privacy options [?]
○ CL mail relay (recommended)
○ no replies to this email

phone/text

☐ show my phone number ☐ phone calls OK ☐ text/sms OK

phone number   extension   contact name

☐ ok for others to contact you about other services, products or commercial interests

c) **What do you have to offer?** Don't feel pressured to offer anything monetary or something material. This can literally be anything; good tunes, travel tips, dad jokes, or information on different star formations.
If you do have gas money or something in material form to offer, include that here. I've learned that not everyone cares if you offer gas money or not, but some people do appreciate it. If you have something else, like hummus that you were gifted or a painting that you made, include that here.

d) **Closing.** To close out the body of your post, say "**Thank you, I look forward to hearing from you**" or something along the same lines, in your own way. You do you!

5. **Rideshare Type:** This is where you'll select "**ride wanted.**"

6. **Contact Information:** You'll enter your email. No worries, people can't see your actual email: they see a CL Mail Relay, which shows them a line of letters and numbers scattered together. I suggest not showing your real email and not entering your phone number.

- To finish up, you'll have to check your email to confirm and publish your post. From there, you'll also be able to find, edit, or delete your post.

- After putting in all this work, you get to sit back and watch the offers hopefully roll in. It can be exciting! Use your judgment when talking to folks about possibilities. Ask questions! Some important things to find out are: Where are they going and when? How do they plan on getting there? How long do they expect the trip to take? Are they expecting anything in return? Have they given rideshares before and have possible contacts of reference?

- **Warning:** Some people may message things that are disturbing, annoying, or simply have nothing to do with ridesharing. It's up to you to choose what you respond to, what you tolerate, and what you will and won't work with.

- **Suggestion:** If possible, try to meet up with the person offering a rideshare before you take off with them in their automobile. Are you able to grab a coffee in the afternoon? Meet them for lunch? Seeing people in person and feeling out their energies can be used to keep yourself safe.

- Once you've found someone suitable offering something that makes sense, solidify the plans and check in regularly. Get their contact information.

- **When you are about to rideshare with someone,** make sure to let a human know where you are, who you're with, and where you're going. Take a picture of the license plate, car, and send the full name of the person that you're with. Let the driver know that you are doing so. Once you're in someone else's car, remember to be mindful of their space.

- **Remember:** If you feel uncomfortable at any point and feel like you need to ditch the situation, do your best to safely do so. Don't stick it out just because you need a ride. There are other options, and you're not able to travel if you're seriously harmed anyway. Always take care of yourself first.

- **Karma Tip:** If you're driving in the future and are able and willing to offer a ride, do so! It puts good energies into your travel bucket. Pass on the love. You can post a ride following the same practice of asking for a ride but choosing "ride offered" instead.

Food for the Brain

I have to tell you the first time that I took a rideshare, I was shaking nervously. I mean, you're getting into a stranger's car, and it can be scary, right? That's why I want to share a few of my own experiences with you and offer some insight as to what ridesharing might be like.

One of the first rideshares I did was completely unplanned. I'm not even sure if it was a rideshare, but more like a desperate hitchhike. It was evening, and I had just crashed my bike down the Blue Ridge Parkway. My bike was smashed, my things scattered, and I had a mild concussion at the time. I was tired, defeated, out of service, physically hurting, and upset. As I stood on the side of the road, trying to flag a car down, I wasn't having much luck. A couple of people stopped, but mainly just to look at the accident scene.

Finally, a family pulled over in an SUV. They had two kiddos and they put me in the back seat between them. They put me in a hotel for the night that was within walking distance of a bike shop. They showed me so much kindness that day—something I hope we would all do for others if we could. That was my first unplanned rideshare. It happened by finding someone going to the same place as me at the moment. It was an amazing experience. There could be times when you feel you don't know how to get to the next place, feel unsafe, or are just frustrated with the seeming lack of options. *Keep on truckin'*!

Another time, I put a rideshare request up, looking from a ride from Missoula, Montana to Portland, Oregon. It was a pretty far stretch, clocking in at about twelve hours in the car. A person with a broken foot responded to me, and they were trying to get from where they were in Missoula to back home in Portland. They were thinking of flying and having someone else drive their car home for them. After conversing, we came to the agreement we'd probably enjoy each other's company, and I could drive the person's car for them. After adding each other on Facebook, and staying in contact every so often, we finally made the trip together. It was fun; we listened to one of my favorite podcasts called *Guys We F*cked*, stopped for cheap gas station snacks, and I even hung out with their mom for a little when we got to Portland, sharing some great conversation. It was a win-win! They saved money on a plane ticket, and I got where I needed to go.

Not every rideshare has been amazing for me—I've felt a little uncomfortable at times. One time, I even got into a heated debate with the person driving the car and decided to pull back a little for my own safety. People who aren't cis, white men: Just by existing, you've probably figured out how you like to handle situations where you feel emotionally or physically threatened by cis, white men. We all have different tactics, ways of working through unsettling situations, and ideas of how we should respond to these potentially dangerous situations. If anything like this ever happens during a rideshare, use your best judgment, and get yourself to safety as quickly as you can.

Overall, even considering every rideshare I've done has been alone and with a man, I've had good experiences. I'll continue using ridesharing, listening to my gut feelings, and practicing safety at the same time.

Safety tips for ridesharing:
- When exchanging conversation and ideas over the internet, never give out your personal information unless you feel absolutely comfortable doing so.
- If you plan to ride with someone but feel uncomfortable or have a bad gut feeling when you meet them, ditch the plan. Make up an excuse, be honest…it doesn't matter to me. Don't move forward with sticky situations.
- Before you start a rideshare, send your location to someone you trust, letting them know where you're headed, when you expect to get there, the full name of the driver, license plate number, and a picture of the car. Stay in communication with your chosen person.

Mantras:
- The universe brings me exactly what I need. There are an abundance of people going in my direction.
- People are willing, able, and excited to help me. I am ready to go on my way!
- I am safe and strong. I protect my energy and body to the fullest extent possible for me.
- I am thankful, but not surprised, when things work out for me.

Resources:
- ***Craigslist Joe***: This is a documentary about a person who, for 31 days (about 1 month) and nights, got everything that he needed from **Craigslist.**
  http://www.craigslistjoe.com/project/about-craigslist-joe/
- ***Race and Gender, Media Bias in Coverage of Missing Persons***: Learn more about the "The Missing White Girl Syndrome" and how race and gender can affect chances of a kidnap happening, being reported, and people being found.
  https://themissingny.nycitynewsservice.com/part-two/race/

4. Traveling By Train

Whoo-hoo, it's time to take a breath! The last few modes of transportation that we discussed and considered were a little lengthy, so let's give the brain a little break and learn how to kick back and relax by train. When I talk about trains in this section, I am referring to trains such as the ones run by the company Amtrak, and not subways or other machines of that sort.

Each experience I've had on a train was a little different, but everyone was relaxing and restful. The cool thing about traveling by train is it's so much more comfortable, breathable, and quieter than traveling by bus, and you can often find it around the same price or cheaper.

Now, before we get into how to get yourself on to a train, we have to discuss how to do this with little money. You have a couple of options here. One, (and you may think I'm joking, but I'm not) you can call the nearest train station and ask them to work for a ticket, or you can walk in and ask. I called a bus station one time to try this. The person who took my call wasn't sure and said that they would talk to a manager, but it sounded like something that could happen. I can't guarantee this will work but it's worth a try.

The second way you could get yourself a train ticket is by buying it. You can use some of the ideas offered in **chapter two**, or, when you get to **chapter six**, you'll learn various ways to make money while on the road. In this chapter, I'll lay out for you, in great detail, how to ask in exchange for the things you need. These are both great options; either coming prepared with some money or working for cash while traveling. With this option, you'll do some type of "work" in exchange for your seat on the train. In this section, we'll walk through what you would do if you decided to buy a ticket online, which is the most common path chosen.

Amtrak

While traveling in the USA, the only long-distance train you'll find is Amtrak. Amtrak has provided me with great experiences so far, as mentioned above. Another great thing about Amtrak is their stations in major cities are accessible to folks with disabilities. They require reservations for accessible space and even offer a ten percent discount for care companions. (3) You can learn more about their station accessibility in the resources below.

I like Amtrak because of the layout of the trains and the headspace offered. They have big, comfortable seats that recline and are usually clean. Lights go out at a certain time and the people on the train are usually quiet and respectful. The bathrooms on the train are pretty decent...way better than the ones you find on buses! There are multiple bathrooms, so you usually don't have to wait long for your turn on the throne.

The coolest thing about Amtrak is their café car. This is part of the train set up like a café, minus the food and beverage counter. In the café car, there are multiple tables of different sizes, chairs, and sofa-like chairs. This is all surrounded by big windows on each side so you can enjoy the views as you glide by.

This is a great space to write, type, read a book, listen to music, daydream, or even strike up a conversation with another passenger. The train cars themselves are also great because they offer storage for your bags, ample walking space in the seating areas, and room to move around and stretch.

As you'll learn below, a quick way to book a ticket with Amtrak is to go directly to their website and we'll walk through doing that together. Another option is going to **www.wanderu.com**, where you can compare bus and train tickets easily. If you put in your place of departure, arrival, and the date, they will compare prices and let you find the cheapest option for your specific trip. If you choose to use this source, you will be booking with whatever transportation company you select but doing it through **Wanderu**. I use **Wanderu** often and would highly suggest checking it out, at least to compare prices.

Bonus: Bikes, instruments, surfboards, and most mobility aids are allowed on Amtrak trains as well!

Specific Baggage Information as of 2021 (4):
Carry-On Baggage:
Each passenger may bring two luggage items, and each item should not exceed 50 lbs. (23 kg) and 28 x 22 x 14 inches each.

Checked Baggage:

Each passenger can check up to 4 bags - 2 free of charge and 2 for $20 per bag, each not to exceed 50 lbs. (23 kg), 75 linear inches (length + width + height).

Special Items:

Baggage over the normal size restrictions or requiring special handling, such as baby items, bicycles, sporting equipment and firearms, may be subject to additional packing requirements and service fees and will be accepted as carry-on and/or checked baggage in lieu of a piece of baggage.

If you are able to work directly for a ticket with Amtrak, then you'll handle all of the trip details and processing directly at the station, or maybe even with someone over the phone. If you're booking online the following directions are for you. There are two places to book tickets, and we'll explore both of them.

- Once you're ready to book a ticket, an option is to head directly online to the Amtrak website. Be prepared to pick an exact day of your departure and the destinations that you'll be leaving from and arriving to.

- On the front page, you'll see spaces to fill out when booking a ticket.

    1. **Ticket Type:** Is this a one-way, round trip, or multi-city ticket? Choose the one that fits your current needs.

    2. **From:** Where are you leaving from? You'll have the choice of choosing your location of departure by searching an exact station, city, or state.

    3. **To:** Where are you headed? You'll have the same choices here. Find the location that you'll be arriving in by selecting an exact station, city, or state.

    4. **Depart:** What is your departure date? Find and select it on the calendar. If you're doing a roundtrip ticket, you'll also be asked to select your return date.

    5. **Traveler:** Is it just you? If so, book a ticket for one.

    6. **Find Trains:** Click on "FIND TRAINS" once you have all of the correct information entered. Make sure that you entered the right month. It feels good and works quicker to get your ticket information right the first time.

    7. **Train Options:** Different trip options will now appear on your screen. I suggest riding coach because this is the cheapest option. This screen will show you how many seats are still available for your selected day, how much they cost, and how long the trip will be. This page also offers extra information on station advisories and baggage.

Coach details (5):

Nonrefundable
No change fees
Two free checked bags
e-Vouchers available
Free Wi-Fi where available
Earn guest reward points

For example, I just searched for a train ticket three days before a specific departure date. I entered the trip details as going from Chicago, Illinois, to Cleveland, Ohio. The cheapest ticket that came up was for a trip that left the station at 6:40 PM and arrived at 1:45 AM the next day. The trip would take 6 hours and 5 minutes, coming in at $48.00.

Hot Tip: The earlier that you know your trip dates and are able to buy tickets, the cheaper they will be, and there will be more seats open on your desired trip.

8. **Add To Cart:** Once you've filled in the bubble for the seat that you want, select **"add to cart."** It will then take you to the next page, asking if you need to add anything else to your trip, like paying for a bicycle or bringing a companion animal.

9. **Login or Continue:** On the next page, you'll have the option of logging in to the Amtrak website or continuing as a guest. Either one works fine. It'll also ask you how you'd like to receive your ticket. If you're online, the only option that shows up is one for an eTicket, and it's free.

10. **Primary Contact Information:** Enter your information here. You'll be asked to provide a first and last name, telephone number, and email address. Make sure that you provide an email that you have access to because this is how they will contact you and where your ticket will be sent.

11. **Travel Protection:** At the bottom of this same page, it'll ask you if you'd like to add travel protection for an extra cost. You can read the details to determine if this is something

that you'd like to do. After this page is filled out, hit **"CONTINUE."**

12. **Payment:** This is where you'll add your credit card information, billing address, and accept the terms and conditions. After you've paid, you'll end on the confirmation page.

- Now that your trip is booked, check your email for your ticket. Make sure to mark it, or put it in a special folder, so that you're able to easily access it. You can also print it out and keep all of your important travel documents together in an envelope or box!

- When you go to the station to catch your train, try to arrive half an hour early at least. I really struggle to do this myself, but it's nice to get there ahead of time and feel confident that you're catching your train and ready to go.

- At the station, you won't have to check in anywhere. If you have questions, find the nearest attendant or find the ticket counter.

- Make sure to find your train and wait in line to get on. As you approach the train, a person will most likely ask to see your ticket and point you in the direction of your car and seat.

- Once you board the train, you can leave big luggage items in the storage space. Take all personal, valuable, and important items with you to your seat.

- Voila, you're ready to go! The train will most likely make stops in different places before it gets to your specific station. Check with the attendants to make sure everything is on schedule and be aware of when you need to prepare to exit the train.

- If you have some sort of alarm, it's helpful to set it a half hour before your estimated time of reaching your stop. This way you have time to prepare; for me that's always looked like waking up, putting my shoes back on, gathering my things, and double checking the space around me to make sure that I don't forget anything.

- When you reach your stop, *triple* check you have all your things and exit the train. And just like that, *boom*, you're there!

Food for the Brain

I have always felt at ease when taking trains. I think it may be the way the train moves softly, and almost more slowly than we're used to, heading to your destination. There is something so yummy about that for me.

And speaking of yummy, Amtrak has a fully plant-based option from their food cart. If you find the spot to grab the grub, make sure you ask for the "vegan" meal. I try to bring my own food because it's much cheaper, but the option is there if you're in need of some calories. Although it wasn't the most amazing thing I had ever had, I was thankful that Amtrak had that option (as they should), and it's available all the time.

Safety tips for taking trains:
- Let someone know where you are boarding the train and where and when you will be arriving.
- If you have valuables with you, keep them above your seat in storage, next to you on the floor, or in your seat. Wrap your bag strap around a part of your body in case someone tries to quickly take it (especially when sleeping).
- If you plan on sleeping, make sure you set an alarm so that you know when to wake up and are ready to exit.
- If you ever feel uncomfortable with where you are, ask an attendant to move your seat and go to another cart.

Mantras:
- I am safe in all forms of transportation.
- This train is protected and moving along right on schedule.

- I make it to my next destination with ease, enjoyment, and relaxation.

Resources:
- ***Making Reservations for Accessible Space | Amtrak***: Make reservations for accessible space and learn more about their guidelines and services.
https://www.amtrak.com/planning-booking/accessible-travel-services/making-reservations-for-passengers-with-a-disability.html

5. Traveling By Bus

Ah, as soon as someone says "bus," my thoughts go right to the good ole Greyhound. In this section, we'll learn why you might want to consider taking a bus, what it might be like, and how to do it.

I have to let you know now I have a love/hate relationship with traveling via bus. Using the bus is a great option because it is usually pretty cheap. On the other hand, they tend to be late, have mechanical problems, and can be uncomfortable and unclean. As we get into some specific companies and what they tend to offer, we'll explore this idea in more detail.

As always, when you're seeking out modes of transportation, check all your options first. I would bet eight out of ten times a bus will be cheaper than traveling via train or by flying, but every once in a while, this isn't the case. This is a good time to go to **www.wanderu.com** to compare prices.

Many ideas can be applied to traveling via bus, as they stand for traveling via train. Let me explain: If you're trying to take a bus without buying a ticket, you have the same options as you did in the section discussing traveling via train. You can call the bus company and ask to work for a ticket, or even enter the station in person and ask to work as a direct exchange.

You also have the option of coming prepared with cash, as presented in **chapter two**, or making it while you're on the road, as shown in **chapter six**. If you're going to try working for a ticket, you'll be following the instructions in **chapter six**. If you're buying a ticket, we'll go over that here. There are two types of buses that are the most popular: Greyhound and Megabus. It is important to note that all Greyhound buses are wheelchair accessible! Greyhound is partnered with essential accessibility, and they provide team members with training in all aspects to work with disabled passengers. You can learn more in the resource section below.

If you find a station close to you, and decide to buy a ticket in person, that's always a great option because there is less of a chance messing up your purchase. Once you're in the station, you can see what it feels like, get your ticket physically, and ask questions to a real human.

If you're buying a ticket online, the procedure is going to look very similar to the one we discussed in the train section. For these steps, we'll use the method it takes to get a seat on the Greyhound. The Megabus website and procedures are similar, so apply the same concepts there if you decide to take a Megabus.

- Once you're ready to book a ticket, the best option is to head directly online to the Greyhound website, found at **www.greyhound.com**, unless you are booking through wanderu.com. Be prepared to pick an exact day of departure and the destinations that you'll be leaving from and arriving to.

- At the top of the page, you'll see a section titled "BOOK A TRIP."

1. **From:** Where are you leaving from? Enter your city, state, or zip code. Click on the location that matches your request.

2. **To:** Where are you headed? Do the same thing, enter your city, state, or zip code. Choose the one that matches your request.

3. **Depart On**: Click on the small calendar to choose your day of departure. After you click on it, make sure the numbers that represent your chosen day are correct.

4. **Add Return:** If you are planning to return to the same place, using the same company, make sure that you add a return date as well. If this is a one-way ticket, leave this space blank.

5. **Passengers:** Under the "from" space, you'll enter how many passengers you're buying a ticket for. If it's just you, make sure it says: "1 Passenger(s)."

6. **Discount Options:** Click on the arrow pointed down to see if you qualify for any discount options. If you do, use that baby!

7. **Search:** When you're all set with the correct location and dates, hit search to see what tickets are available.

8. **Choose Your Outgoing Trip:** Different trip options will now appear on your screen. I suggest riding economy because this is the cheapest option. This screen will show you different days that offer different prices, how much they cost, and how long the trips will be.

Economy Details as of 2021 (6):
1 Checked Bag Free
2nd and 3rd bag 42.00 each
Non-Refundable
$20.00 Fee to Change Date/Time Before Trip Date
Earn 1 Road Reward Point Each Way

For example, I just searched for a bus ticket, two days before my desired departure date. I entered the trip details as going from Chicago, Illinois, to Cleveland, Ohio. The cheapest ticket that came up was for a trip that left the station at 7:30 AM and arrived at 4:15 PM. The trip would take 7 hours and 45 minutes, coming in at $41.00.

9. **Sort By:** At the top right of the page, you can filter your searches to easily find what you're looking for. You have the options of seeing the Earliest Departure, Cheapest, or Fastest first. I always go with the cheapest when I travel and work as I go.

10. **View Itinerary:** While you're deciding which bus trip you want to take you can see their full itineraries by clicking on this button. The full schedule will pop up and it'll show every single stop, starting with your departing location, and ending with your destination. It'll let you know the exact location where you'll be stopping, the exact time that the stop will happen, how long the stop will last, and what the station is like. On some stops, you'll get off the bus completely and transfer to a new bus.

11. **Book this Fare:** Once you've found your bus, fill in the dot above the price of the bus. A new button will pop up that says: "BOOK THIS FARE." Click on it and it'll take you to your next step.

12. **Passenger Details, 1 Adult:** Fill in your first and last name.

13. **Payment Details:** select "CREDIT OR DEBIT CARD." If you select "CASH," then you'll have to find a local station to go pay for your ticket.

14. **Primary Cardholder Details:** Select your name. If you are gifting a ticket to someone, or someone is gifting a ticket to you, the company may charge you an extra fee. My ticket showed up as $18.00. You'll see a box to your right that has your ticket summary and cost. Make sure it's correct. Enter your credit card number, CVV, and expiration date.

15. **Contact Details:** Here, you'll enter your address, zip code, city, state, country, phone number, and email so they know where to send your ticket and any important information. Be sure to enter an email address you can access.

16. **Ticket Options:** Are you going to print your ticket, or pick it up at the station? Now is the time to decide.

Hot Tip: Print out your ticket ahead of time. More than once I have planned to pick up a ticket at the station, and it's been closed, leaving me on the curb. It can be challenging to change the method of receiving your ticket after you've selected it, so think through it completely. Important: If you print your ticket, you'll need a matching photo ID to get on the bus. If you are choosing to pick up your ticket at the station, call the local station to make sure it is open when you plan to pick it up, whether that's a couple days ahead of time, or the day of. If you plan to print it, there are a couple of places to get it printed. If you're staying with a host, ask them to help you print it. Even if they don't have a printer, they may know someone who does. If you are not staying with a host, check out the local library. They'll let you print things, and you pay them in cash or change. If the library is not an option, search for local shipping and printing centers.

17. **Pay Now:** After you've agreed to the Terms and Conditions, hit pay now. Your payment will be processed, and they will email you with information about your journey. Remember, **they usually will not accept your email confirmation in place of a ticket**. They most often will not let you on the bus without a ticket.

- On the day of your departure, call the Greyhound station and see if the buses are running on time. They often are not, and you could find yourself sitting in the station for hours, or outside of it.

- When you're ready to go, make sure you have your ticket and arrive at least a half hour early. Greyhound buses are usually running behind, so you may be waiting for a good chunk of time. Bring a book! May I suggest *Women Who Run with the Wolves: Myths and Stories of the Wild Woman Archetype* by Clarissa Pinkola Estés?

- When you arrive at the station, get your ticket, if needed, and wait for your bus. If you have large luggage which is not a carry-on, make sure to go to the ticket counter and check it. They will put a tag on your bag and give you a ticket as well. Greyhound is strict about checking this. If your bag is not checked, they may not let you on, even if you have a ticket.

- Make sure you are waiting at the right terminal and listen to announcements. When you are ready to go, make sure you have all of your items. Your bigger luggage will go under the bus. Make sure to take all of your important items, cash, and valuables with you in your carry-on.

- Once on the bus, find a seat that looks safe and comfortable. Sometimes the buses are crowded, and you'll have to sit with another human you don't know. If for any reason during your trip you feel uncomfortable, let the bus driver know. If you are sitting with someone you don't know, it may be helpful to ask to sit on the outside so you can leave as quickly if needed.

- If you plan on sleeping, make sure your valuables are in a safe place. Wrapping an item's strap around part of your body may help you become alert if someone tries to take it. Set an alarm a half hour before your next stop. Greyhound drivers are usually pretty vocal, so they'll probably be just as effective as getting you up as your alarm.

- Before getting off the bus, make sure you're in the right place, and you have all your belongings. Don't forget your luggage under the bus.

As a side note, Greyhound buses are often cold! I like to keep a jacket, blanket, and/or sleeping bag with me while I'm on the bus. Even during the summer, I've never once felt too warm on the bus. Greyhound buses also stop very frequently. They give you breaks to stretch, grab food, and use the restroom. During long trips you may be switching buses frequently. Pay attention to the itinerary on your ticket and any changes announced by the bus driver!

Bikes on the Bus

If you're traveling with a bike and need to bring it on the bus, this may be a possibility. If you're traveling with Greyhound, they tell you that your bike needs to be in a box, and that you'll be paying an extra fee for it. The reason I am not including their exact words in this section is they don't really specify, and I've been told different things at different times from the company.

When I did my bike tour I took my bike on a Greyhound bus with me a few times. I called the company to ask for the policy on bikes and was told different things during different calls. One thing is for sure, though: your bike will need to be in a box.

Now, you don't necessarily need to take it apart to put it in a box. When I took my bike with me, I found cardboard in dumpsters and used duct tape to fit the cardboard to my bike so that it was completely covered. Yes, this was a little bit of a hassle, but no, I did not know how, nor did I have the tools to take my bike apart and put it back together. If you do, more power to you!

Each time I got on the bus, the driver gave me a funny look and a good scoff but loaded my bike. I know that people react differently in different situations, so be prepared for various outcomes.

You'll have to check your bike in the box, so don't forget to do that. I've been charged money for my bike sometimes, and not charged at other times. Greyhounds can be wishy-washy, so you never quite know what you're going to get. I still recommend using them if you have the energy for it!

- If you're trying to take a bike onto the bus, make sure you have it boxed up. This can be taken apart, or just taping a box to the outside and hoping that they'll accept it. It doesn't always work though!

- Call the station that you're leaving from to learn about their policy on bikes.

Now, let's talk about our other bus option:

I've never tried to take a bike on the Megabus but found some words from some folks who did. Megabus states on their website that their policy is as such as of 2021 (7): **"Megabus does not check luggage** or provide receipts for luggage transported on the bus by the passenger. Customers are advised that Megabus will accept up to ONE (1) piece of luggage per passenger reservation. For guidance, this must not exceed 62 inches when adding the total exterior dimensions of the piece (length + width + height) and should not weigh more than 50 pounds. Passengers can also take on board one (1) small carry-on bag that will fit in the overhead storage compartments or under the seat."

On **bikepgh.org**, one person writes: "I took a bike (no box) on Megabus recently from Columbus to Pittsburgh. The driver let me put it on because he didn't seem to care one way or another about any policy. When I got to PGH though, the Megabus attendants at the convention center rather aggressively told me I could never do it again." (8)

So, as you can see, I can't tell you one way or another. Some folks may let it slide while others won't. Call the local Megabus station for more details before your trip.

Food for the Brain

Oh, Greyhound. I have always had the most interesting experiences on your buses. I've taken these buses more times than I can count on one hand, maybe even two, and would say I am ready for anything now. What I'm sharing here is not to deter you from taking the Greyhound, but to give you an idea of what you may experience. Like I said before, Greyhounds are often full, and you have to sit next to another human you don't know. Sometimes, this is wonderful. I've had a couple of experiences where I ended up sitting next to some awesome people and had some great and engaging conversations.

One time, I sat next to someone who I met in the station, around my own age. We have similar goals when it comes to travel and making a career out of it, so we discussed starting projects together. During our long bus ride, we bonded over similar interests and new sparks with travel ideas.

On a couple of rides, though, I sat with or near men who did not want to end the conversation at any point. I always say "hey" to the person sitting next to me and introduce myself if it seems as if they want more interaction. After doing this with a couple of folks, I knew what to expect in the future. They seemed very driven to get my name, phone number, social media links, and question me about my current relationship status. I'm all about meaningful conversation, but a couple of times I felt it was way too much and too invasive. I did things like putting my earphones in and letting them know that I was zoning out, or going to sleep, and they still didn't take a hint.

I have other friends who have experienced the same things, and each one handles it differently. It seems to me, if you feel safe in saying this, the best option is to just tell the other person you are not interested in the conversation at hand, and you would want to be left alone.

On that very same first Greyhound trip, I came off the bus feeling like I had just lived out a lifetime in the seat. I saw people form relationships very quickly over a couple of hours, people in conflict screaming at each other and taking up a lot of emotional space, and kids getting sick and throwing up all over the bus. As I said, the Greyhound has always been an experience!

One of the most memorable experiences I had on a bus took place in Chile. I arrived as an inexperienced traveler and exchange student for the year. My host parents went to a larger city to visit family, and for some reason, trusted me with the task of taking the bus a little later than them, alone, to meet up with them there. I can't forget to mention I only knew a few phrases in Spanish and had no internet connection. So, I boarded a bus, alone, ready to take on the task of navigating a completely new place while not understanding a lick of what anyone was saying.

My brain was so worn out from all of the new experiences and learning that I fell asleep on the bus. I later woke up to the dark inside of the terminal, at the end of the bus line, in a passenger-less bus. The bus driver caught me out of the corner of their eye while trying to exit the bus and realized I had missed my stop. They tried to tell me where we were and what was going on in Spanish, but since I didn't understand anything and was in a sleepy haze, I started crying. (You might catch on to the trend of me and tears throughout this guide!)

The driver quickly understood I couldn't understand anything they said and couldn't read the signs around us. After unsuccessfully trying to communicate and come up with a plan, I gave up and called my host dad, who I also didn't understand at the time. I handed the phone to the driver and let them work it out. It turned out I was in the right city but way past my stop. The driver took the bus back out of the terminal and met my host dad at a random bus stop. I felt completely out of control, useless, and lost the whole time. Even with all of those heavy feelings ruling the story, I can still look back and laugh, instead of cry, at my mishaps and unwanted adventures!

Safety tips for taking the bus:
- Be aware of your body and possessions in bus stations and on the bus.
- Consider taking mace with you.
- Check your itinerary before starting your bus trip. It is good to know when the bus stops, when you'll be allowed breaks, and when you'll arrive at your destination.
- If you feel uncomfortable with a conversation you're having with someone, or where you're sitting, move to a new seat. If the person follows you uninvited, let the bus driver and those around you know.
- Set an alarm on your phone if you plan to sleep on the bus so you don't miss your stop.
- Let someone know where you are on your route and check in often to let them know you are safe.

Mantras:
- Transportation works smoothly and easily for me.
- I get where I need to go and feel safe doing so.
- I travel with ease and protection.
- Every bus I get on has an excellent driver and wonderful passengers.

Resources:
- *Greyhound Bus Services to People with Disabilities | Disabled World*: Learn more about services provided to disabled folks while traveling with Greyhound.
  https://www.disabled-world.com/disability/transport/public/greyhound-buses.php#:~:text=All%20Greyhound%20buses%20are%20wheelchair,vision%20and%20age%2Drelated%20disabilities

6. Driving for Others

As we continue down the list, I'll share all of my ideas that are the freest before we get to more expensive ones. In this section, we'll talk about driving cars for others. This won't be a large section as we already talked about how you may end up driving someone else's car through **Craigslist**. This section is less about explaining how to do it, and more about letting you know this is an option.

People need their cars driven for various reasons: they are injured and cannot drive but need to get somewhere, they are moving and want someone to drive their car while they drive another vehicle, or they might just want someone to drive for them on a cross country trip because they don't feel they can do it all themselves. Who knows...it really could be anything!

There are a couple of ways you may find someone who needs their car driven across the USA. This isn't something that you can often plan well, but more something that pops up, and may just work out for you.

This is a good option if you're looking to travel with a small budget, as people will often give you gas money if they're in big need of transferring their car. If not, you may have to find some cash to pay for gas as you go from one place to another.

Craigslist

This strange spot on the internet, Craigslist, seems to be the number one place to run into someone who needs their car driven across the USA.

- Just as you did for creating a Rideshare, in **option #3** of this section, you'll need to get on Craigslist and check out what's going on in the Rideshare section. Keep your eyes open for people who may need assistance in getting their vehicle from one place to another. It happens!

- Create a post in the Rideshare section, and let people know you are willing to drive a car for them, if they're moving, need help, etc.

- Use the same structure we used for posting an ad in Rideshare but tweak it to fit your story and travel needs.

Network

This is pretty simple. If you are willing to drive someone's car for them, let people know. Ask around. It may seem like you're searching for a needle in the haystack, but I promise travel magic is real, and sometimes it works out.

- Post a rough estimate on your social media accounts of when and what direction you'll be heading. Let people know you are willing to drive their vehicles, if anyone is in need.

- Keep your ears open in travel spaces and your everyday conversations. Opportunities for you to drive for someone else may show up.

If you do end up driving someone else's car, please be respectful, careful, and considerate. Leave the vehicle in the same condition, or even better, when you're finished!

Safety tips for driving for others:
- When posting on social media or Craigslist, never tell people exactly when and where you're going. This can be done through direct and private messages when you are working out the details.
- Use common sense and be careful when making exchanges with humans through Craigslist. If something doesn't feel right, don't do it.
- Make sure the car you're driving has insurance for all drivers or you are covered yourself. You don't want to end up paying if you get pulled over or have an accident. If the owner of the vehicle is not present with you while you are driving, have them sign a notarized letter giving their consent about your agreement.
- When you are driving someone's car, be cautious and drive with care. Let someone know where you are leaving from and headed to. Be sure to check in during your travels.

Mantras:
- I easily, and safely, get where I need to go.
- The perfect form of transportation is readily available to me.
- The world is full of perfect travel opportunities, and I am ready to receive what works best for me.
- Every vehicle that I operate runs smoothly and functions perfectly. I arrive safely where I need to go.

7. Hitchhiking

Yes folks, we're here: hitchhiking. Although I've only hitchhiked a handful of times, and am itching to do it more, I spent a lot of time around other travelers who do it often. Obviously, hitchhiking is riskier than most modes of transportation for many reasons: One, you're standing by the side of the road while waiting for rides, and it could put your physical body in danger if a driver makes a wrong move. Two, when someone picks you up, you have no idea who they are, or what intentions they may have. Three, once you're in the car, you may not have the same control over where you go, when you stop, and how you move. There's a big risk if you're considering hitchhiking, but we'll go over some precautions to make it a safer experience.

One thing to keep in mind is in some areas it's illegal to hitchhike. I'm not saying all laws are right or even deserve respect, but it's good to know when you may have to deal with police. I've never heard of anyone getting punished for hitchhiking, but you never know what will happen in the hands of the law. Usually, people get asked to move. Before you start hitchhiking, look up the laws of the areas so you're aware, even if you don't plan on following them.

A fun benefit of hitchhiking is it doesn't require technical planning. You head out the road and find a way to get where you need to go. Also, it's usually free, because chances are no one is going to ask you to buy a ticket or even pay for gas money. If you're planning on hitchhiking, there are a few things you need to do before, during, and after you get into someone's car.

- Consider making a sign. Find a writing tool and paper, plastic, or cardboard to write on. I suggest looking around for scrap material or checking out the dumpsters. Get crafty.

  Although a sign is not required, it will help people know where you're going, and speed up their decision on whether or not to pick you up. If they can clearly see you're going in the same direction as them, they may be more inclined to offer a ride.

- When you're ready to hitchhike, let someone know what your plan is. Then you'll have to find a good spot to hitch from.

  To do this, you'll want to be on the side of the road you plan on starting from, or on the ramp leading to a road. You'll need to position yourself facing the traffic going in your desired direction.

  Make sure you position yourself in a place where it is easy for people to pull over. If you're standing randomly at the side of a highway, people will be going too fast to stop, even if they would like to. Be cautious and smart when picking your starting area.

  If you have items with you, make sure they are out of the road and out of the way. Keep them close by so you can grab them easily when you're ready to go, but make sure they aren't putting any drivers at risk.

- When you've found your ideal area, hold up your sign or your thumb. Let people know you need something, or else they may think that you're just standing by the side of the road.

Make eye contact with the people driving by. If it looks like you don't care and aren't paying attention, they may not care to pull over.

- Be patient. It may take 20 seconds to get picked up, or it may take 20 minutes. Remember: No one *has* to pick you up, but with all the cars and people moving in the world, hopefully someone will.

If you've been in one spot for too long, consider moving to a different spot and trying again there.

- Once someone pulls over, don't automatically assume you will be traveling with them. Use caution. Head over to the car and stop a few feet away. Ask the driver where they are headed and calculate if it will be helpful to you or not to go with them.

Follow your instincts. If it doesn't feel right, **<u>DON'T</u>** do it. It's not worth it. Listen to gut reactions, and what your body and spirit are telling you. Feel out the driver's energy. Have your mace in your hand for safety!

If you don't want to get into the car, simply respond and decline. You have a few options here. One, you can be honest and say that you don't want to go with them. In my generally femme-perceived body, and my mind concerned with safety politics, I usually go with a softer approach. The other option would be to say you're not needing to go the same way. If they continue to press, say *"no thank you"* and walk away from the car. Three, you can tell them plans have changed (play it out by looking at your phone) and someone you know is actually coming to pick you up.

As you can see, you can be blunt here, or get creative and craft a story. The important thing is you're working in a way where you feel protected and as safe as possible in any given situation. If you do want to go with a person that has pulled over, take a few safety measures first:

1. Take a picture of the license plate, or write it down, and send it to someone who is aware of what you are doing.
2. Before you get in the car, ask the driver for their name, and consider asking to take a picture of them as well. Send this information to the same person.
3. Confirm your plans. Make sure they are going in the same direction they originally told you.
4. Be aware of the space around you. What is in the car? What does the energy feel like?
5. If you have any weapons or objects that can be used to protect yourself (such as mace, a knife, or a taser), keep them close to you.

- What happens from here is what you and the driver make of it. Share as much as you feel like sharing and let yourself have a blast if you're digging the situation!

- If you feel like you need to exit the situation at any moment while you're in the car, speak up and ask the driver to pull over and let you out. Another good place to bail is at any stops, such as stops at gas stations or red lights. Do not hesitate to open the door and get out if you feel unsafe.

- When you get safely to your destination, thank the driver if you feel inclined to do so, and let your trusted person know you are safe.

Hitchhiking is a different experience for everyone, but we all need to consider the seriousness of the danger we could put ourselves in. Depending on who we are, and how we present ourselves, we all can create our own rules and regulations we follow for safety during hitchhiking.

Food for the Brain

As someone who is not a cisgender, heterosexual, white man, I am extra cautious of who I get into a car with. This could be a long and complicated conversation, as the subject is also very complex. But, as a general rule, I only get in the car with men if I am with a large group of people hitchhiking. If I am alone, I don't do it. What you do is up to you! I keep in mind my safety is most important, and there is always another way. There is always another ride.

Although we've talked about a lot of safety issues, I personally haven't heard any horror stories from my hitchhiking friends yet. One of my friends is 19 years old and already an experienced hitchhiker. She's been in the car with various people and has had nothing but good and interesting stories to tell from her experiences. I interviewed her on my podcast and her full hitchhiking adventure story can be found in the resources below! I recommend checking it out if you want a more in-detail idea of what hitchhiking might be like.

Out of the handful of times I hitchhiked, I was with another person, and it was pretty fun. When I was an exchange student in Chile, myself and two friends were meeting others for a hike but didn't want to pay a taxi to get there. So, we just stood by a busy road and held out our thumbs. It actually took longer than I expected to get picked up, but an older man finally pulled over and picked us up. (Sorry, mom!) We spent the rest of the car ride singing, giggling, and enjoying our adventurous spirits together.

In 2017 I was hiking with my friend in Yellowstone National Park. We were a couple of miles away from our car, on top of a hill, when it started to storm. We didn't feel safe with a powerful storm rolling in so we decided to end our hike early. That left us a couple of miles away from the vehicle and out in the open. We picked a spot by the side of the road and stuck the thumbs out. Even though it's illegal to hitchhike in most national parks, some service vehicles drove by and saw us without saying anything. Again, practice care around your personal privilege and feelings of safety. We eventually got picked up by an RV full of Danish folks who were rich in spirit and excited to take care of us during our short time together. They offered us water and snacks, asked us questions about our travels, and let us know we could use their restroom if needed. It was a pleasant interaction, and it was a memorable way to end our hike.

You can sometimes come across folks who want to help, encourage, and support you (even if they don't know you). Those are the folks you are looking to ride with, and I hope those are the ones that pull over to pick you up.

Safety tips for hitchhiking:
- Choose a spot by the road when hitchhiking which puts you and other drivers in the least amount of danger.
- Remember you don't have to get into any vehicle that stops. Be selective.
- Carry a weapon on you such as mace, a taser, or pepper spray. If you don't have a weapon, look around you and see what might be used as one such as a glass bottle, a pen, or anything you can use to protect yourself in a worst-case scenario.
- Get a photo of the license plate number, or write it down, and get the driver's name before getting in the car. If you are able to send their information to someone else via text, do so. Check in with this person once you have safely arrived at your destination.
- Hitchhike with one or more people if possible.

- Follow your intuition and gut feelings. If it's telling you not to get in a car, or to exit as quickly as possible, do so.
- Be aware of local hitchhiking laws to minimize interaction with police.

Mantras:
- I am physically safe at all times. I feel a bubble of energy forming around me, protecting me from outside influences.
- I get picked up in a timely manner. Everyone is right on time.
- Everyone who stops for me has good intentions and follows through with them. Each driver is cautious, mindful, and respects my space.
- I am grateful for all of the help I continuously receive. I easily get where I need to go.

Resources:
- ***#11 I Just Decided to Hitchhike | National Parks, Jail Time, and Sky Diving*:**
  This resource is hands down my most favorite podcast episodes I've recorded. Nicole tells us all about her hitchhiking adventure—offering you insight as to what it might be like and how to master the art.
  https://soundcloud.com/unrulystories/hitchhiking-adventures

8. Driving for Yourself

If you have a vehicle, or can get your hands on one, you always have the option to drive yourself and take an epic road trip. I'll admit, this is a hard option to pursue in a way that is absolutely free. Let me start out by saying the book titled *Steal This Book* by Abbie Hoffman is an excellent resource on how to make this happen by getting free gas. I'll leave it at it.

If you decide to drive around the country, and aren't using Abbie's methods, you'll have to consider gas costs and any extra repairs that could add up. If you already have enough to pay for your gas, it could be smooth sailing. You don't necessarily have to have enough money for extra repairs, as nothing may ever need to be repaired on your vehicle. But remember, extra charges may come up when driving. Some of these include toll roads, speeding tickets, insurance, and covering any other malfunctions.

You could work as you go, making money to pay for gas before moving onto your next place. We'll learn how to do that in **chapter six.** You would also then have that dough to cover extra vehicle expenses.

Another way to cut down trip costs while driving is to ask folks to pay for your gas as you travel. I haven't personally done it, so I can't speak from first-hand experience. But I have heard of and talked to other travelers who have used this method of getting around. People have told me they pull up at gas stations and ask others to pay for their gas while they're filling their own cars. If you go this route, consider sharing your travel story. You never know who will want to help out!

Although some people might have a knee-jerk reaction against this, I like the idea. You are literally and simply asking for what you need. If someone wants to cover your gas and meet your needs, they have the opportunity to do so. If they don't want to, they don't have to. It's as simple as that. The following tips all come from my road trips across the USA, including the two month trip my partner and I did in 2021 from North Carolina to Washington, and then back in my van!

- Find a vehicle you can maneuver. Decide how you will pay for gas; this could be a combination of multiple things and could change over time.

- Decide if you are planning your route, or not. Remember this is always subject to change, and it's up to you to decide how much planning you want to do.

- Are you going to change the inside of the vehicle? Maybe you have an RV, camper, or something else that already has a live-in setup inside. If not, consider building a cheap and simple set up of a bed, storage space, and some sort of table. My partner and I did all these things in my van using scrap material and paint for less than $5.00.

- Load your car with the items you need. To avoid potentially putting yourself in legal trouble, make sure you have your license and proof of insurance with you.

- It is completely optional, but I suggest having some sort of GPS or map. You could possibly use the GPS on your phone, get your hands on some paper maps, or buy or borrow someone else's GPS. Another option is looking for used ones on the internet; **Craigslist** and **eBay** are great places for that.

- Ideally, you may want to get your vehicle inspected before you go. You may not if funds won't cover it at the moment or if it's not a concern to you.

- Use caution while driving. Be present and alert. Pull over if you are too tired to drive! Don't risk it.

- If you are in public and looking for a place to park for the night, try to find an area that feels safe. This could include parking on the side of a street, in a friend's or stranger's driveway (with permission) or finding a parking lot that feels comfortable. Walmart parking lots and other big name, earth-destroying businesses are generally open for overnight guests, so keep that in mind as you go.

While on a two-month road trip in my van with my partner in 2021, we found some excellent resources for free parking. One of them is the **Park4Night** app, and the other is **FreeCampsites.net**. They both allow you to find free overnight parking and camping spots in your area and read reviews by those who have stayed there before! We also took advantage of Bureau of Land Management (BLM) land and those spots often ended up being our favorites. I'll explain what "BLM land" is in **chapter four**!

- If you're at a national park or on back roads, use discretion when choosing a place to park overnight. Remember national park rangers are helpful when it comes to finding parking and camping spots close to the park. While on our 2021 road trip, we always called the park to ask where the best free camping was located. They were always happy to explain the views and set up the camping areas in the park you must pay for. I've written blog post guides on a handful of national parks and listed the link in the resources below. If you ask the locals, make sure you don't give out too much information. Practice safety and don't let them know exactly where you will be.

- If you're sleeping in your car at night, make sure to hide your valuables, and keep the doors locked. Be cautious and make sure that you have the right amount of airflow in your car throughout the night so you can breathe. Make sure all cooking gear is shut off and no toxic fumes are filling up your vehicle overnight. If you have mace or other protection, consider having it near you while you are sleeping.

In addition to these instructions, there are some pros and cons I would like to discuss with you about driving for yourself, I have felt through personal experience.

Pros:
- You are able to feel quite sure you have a way to get around. You won't have to book tickets, pay for rides, or experience having to figure out your next way of getting where you need to go.

- You will always have a place to stay. It could be frustrating, or even scary at times when you don't know where you'll lay your head for the night. If you have your own vehicle, you're always covered as long as you can find a secure parking spot.
- You are mostly in control of where you're going, when you leave, and how long it takes to get there. You don't have to wait for rides or be at the mercy of others.
- You are able to take other people with you. If you are traveling with your own vehicle, you may have space if you find that there are others that you would like to travel with.
- You are able to carry more physical items with you that you may need or want.

Cons:
- You have to find a way to cover car expenses, which can be pretty high in certain situations.
- You may not meet as many people as you would if you were traveling through other modes of transportation. Because of the reliability of a car, you probably won't have to reach out to others for assistance as often or have the opportunity of meeting and spending time with completely new people, as you would on a bus or train.
- You may not feel as high a level of adventure as you would if you had to find different ways to get around constantly. This can be a pro or a con, depending on who you are. This method of travel might be the safest option for many. For me, personally, part of the excitement of travel is figuring it out as I go and meeting new spirits along the way. When I drive, I feel as if I don't have as big of a window of opportunity for that because I have a way to get around, and a place to stay. I am then less likely to reach out and ask to stay with others, or see as many new faces throughout my day.

Food for the Brain

I did my first cross-country road trip by car in 2018. You can listen to a summary of that exciting and funky trip with the link listed in the resources section. I've also spent a little bit of time living in my van behind a garage. I recently spent two months traveling across the USA in my van and have learned some nifty tips and tricks for those who will be spending a lot of time in their vehicle!

During my first trip across the USA, I used a bike as my main mode of transportation. Along the way, I met some really awesome humans with whom I wanted to travel. Biking just wasn't going to happen for them and I wanted a break. So, we got into their cars and took off road tripping together. It was honestly great! We went through different national parks, sang in the car, and were able to travel long distances on our own time. We had the freedom and flexibility to do what we wanted.

On one trip, I ended up heading out of Portland, Oregon with someone I had been talking to through the Couchsurfing app. I didn't know him beforehand, but we ended up really enjoying each other's company. Our original plan was to take a couple of day trips together in the car that he had rented. We visited the coast of Oregon, stopping to

explore little towns, and went on some beautiful hikes in nature. At the end of a long day of exploring, we decided it was time for both of us to feel the cold water that climbs onto the shore of the West Coast. We stripped down on an already extremely chilly day and went wild with the rush of the iciness of the water. After returning to Portland, he offered for me to travel with him on the next leg of my trip. He was

heading to Crater Lake. Considering our previous experience together, I decided to go with him.

When it was time to leave Portland, we packed up my bike and shoved it into the back seat. We drove to Crater Lake National Park, exchanging stories of our lives as we went. He was from Switzerland and was also an engineer, super savvy with numbers, math, and science. He made a good amount of money, and traveled often, seeing a lot of the world, with more traditional comfort. If you know me at all, you'll find that his lifestyle and experiences were very different from mine, so I truly enjoyed my time with him.

After jumping into the cold water of Crater Lake and chasing sunrises by running up the snowy mountainsides, we decided to get cozy and head into a little town nearby. After using a hotel for its water and heat, we watched some folks outside that were dancing, cheering,

and celebrating by the big lake which sat close to the buildings and campsites. We grabbed cream sodas from a tiny convenience store and sat by the water, laughing at the adventures and mishaps we experienced during our time together.

That night we really wanted to find a place to stay, indoors; it was cold, dark, and we hadn't totally defrosted from the day well-spent outside. All of the hotels and campsites were either full, or super expensive, so we decided to sleep in the car. We parked in a dirt lot behind the cabins on the same property as the hotel and made room in the small car by hiding my bike inside of the claw of a bulldozer. It was a long night; it was cold inside the car, making it hard to fall asleep. When the next morning came, I had never felt so happy and relieved to feel the sun. I was thankful we had a car. We were able to use it as a place to rest, a way to cover large distances, and do things on our own time.

During the same bike trip, I met someone who instantly became a friend and travel partner through Couchsurfing. I had taken a bus to Nashville, Tennessee, and didn't know I would have a break that lasted all night, before I could take the next bus. As I arrived in the city, I frantically sent out messages on the Couchsurfing app, explaining my situation and almost begging for a place to stay.

Someone responded within the hour of my request and was there to pick me up within fifteen minutes. It turned out my host was a traveling soul like myself and, at that time, had a serious itch to get out and go somewhere. After hanging out all evening and bonding over vegan pizza, I expressed wanting to skip the states between me and Colorado and head straight there.

Neither of us had ever been to Colorado, but we both had a burning desire to go. The next day I caught my bus and headed to Kentucky to continue biking. After a couple of weeks of touring, my previous host, and now friend, met me in Illinois. From there, he phoned his new job and called in sick. Sick of going through the motions and grinding away, that is. We threw my bike in the back seat and headed straight for Colorado!

Some of my fondest memories from that trip were times when we were both tired and almost sick of driving. We were taking turns, driving on and off, to be able to have him back home within two days after reaching Colorado together. One night, we had to get some rest, so we pulled over behind a Chipotle. We went dumpster diving for chips and guac and found some food in questionable condition. I quickly fell asleep outside under a streetlight on the grass in my sleeping bag. Within a few hours I woke up, went on a run at sunrise and used the sprinklers as a shower I felt was much needed.

We kept going making it all the way to Rocky Mountain National Park, the Garden of the Gods, Colorado Springs, and Denver. After our adventures in Colorado, I was dropped off in a town nearby to continue on my biking journey. Although it was all a whirlwind, it's one of the best road trips that I've ever experienced in my life. If you're ready hear me tell this story, *the full story*, listen to the podcast episode listed below in the resources. You won't regret it!

Safety tips for driving yourself:
-   To stay out of legal trouble and minimize interaction with the police, consider having a license and form of insurance with you.
-   Have some sort of map or guide to help you get around if this feels necessary to you.
-   Do not drive under the influence of substances—it could cost your life, along with the lives of others.
-   If you're sleepy, pull over. If someone else is driving, make sure that they are awake and feeling capable of driving at all times. Rolling down the windows and singing loudly are good ways to keep yourself, or another driver, awake! Bring an essential oil like peppermint to inhale when you need a boost, or lavender for calming effects and to reduce anxiety.
-   When parking somewhere overnight, hide your valuables and lock your doors. Make sure you feel safe in the chosen parking area and you can breathe during the night by leaving cracks in the windows. Keep mace near you while sleeping.

Mantras:
- I am a skilled and confident driver. I am alert, focused, and calm while driving.
- My vehicle is always a safe place. Other drivers are alert, focused, and careful while driving around me.
- I am always safe with a place to stay and a way to get around; my vehicle assists me on my journeys.

Resources:
- ***Steal This Book*** *by Abbie Hoffman*: Learn how to always find, or take, free gas to keep you going!
  https://firestorm.coop/products/1046-steal-this-book.html
- ***How We Found Free Camping/Parking Spots While Traveling The U.S. In Our Van***: This is a detailed post on my website that will tell you all that you need to know when it comes to finding free camping and parking spots!
  http://wanderwoman.online/index.php/2021/03/08/free-parking-and-camping-usa/
- National Park Guides: This link will take you to a page on my website that displays all of the guides that I've created for National Parks up to date.
  http://wanderwoman.online/index.php/category/travel-destinations/national-park-guides-travel-destinations/
- ***#38 When the Travel Bug Bites: Unruly Travel Tales By Calen Otto***: Listen to the full story of my trip across the USA by bike in exciting detail.
  https://soundcloud.com/unrulystories/travelbug-part-3

9. Flying

This section will not be as long because you will have to put more time and research into this yourself if you consider flying as a mode of travel. One thing to recognize is each airline operates differently and has their own rules and regulations. If you want to travel by plane, you have a couple of options for getting a plane ticket. Some are more expensive, some take more time and energy, and some require you to be creative.

Traveling by plane is great because you can cross large bodies of land or water in a shorter amount of time compared to other modes of travel. The downside is it's one of the harsher options on the environment. My first inclination is to say flying is more expensive, but sometimes you can find a cheaper ticket that is less than a bus or train ticket. If you're wanting to travel a large distance in a short amount of time, or cross a large body of water, flying is the way to go.

You have a few ways of getting your hands on a ticket. One, you can use different methods of work as you go, as explained in **chapter seven**, to make money as you go and then buy a plane ticket. Two, you can call the company of choice and ask to work for a ticket. I've never tried this personally and don't see it working out often...but you never know. It's worth a shot!

Three, you can use points with an airline in exchange for a ticket. If you're in the game of having a credit card connected to an airline, building up points as you shop, you can cash them in for miles. Does anyone around you use this point system and have extra miles to give? Consider phoning a friend. Ask someone you know who shops a lot, has a lot of money, or owns a business to give you the points they earn to exchange for tickets. You could also make a post on social media letting friends know you need a ticket.

Four, you can buy your plane ticket. Maybe it's through cash you already have, but either way you'll want to search online to find the best deals. If you've found other ways to fly for free, please send me a love letter and let me know how!

- With your desired travel dates in mind, find a website that compares prices to offer you the best deals. You can do this by simply searching "cheap plane tickets" through **Google**, or by using my recommended sites.

I'm listing these three sites because, through my personal experience, I always find the lowest prices here. I like to use **www.cheapoair.com**, **momondo.com**, and **justfly.com**. All three websites are committed to finding you the cheapest plane tickets for your selected dates and showing you all of your options with different airlines.

Hot Tip: When using these websites or their apps, remember to set price alerts so they can contact you when the price of your desired ticket drops. Sometimes when I've set them, I've been alerted each day of a price drop. It's a great way to save money without the hassle of checking back every few days.

- When you choose a site that fits you best, you'll be asked to enter where you're leaving from, where your destination is, and the date you'll be leaving. Make sure to enter the correct information and indicate whether you're searching for a round-trip or one-way ticket.

- After you've entered your information, let the website search for you. Your only job is to look over the flights it presents and decide which one is for you.

- Once you've found a flight, you'll have to enter payment information and other personal information. This is similar to the process we discussed buying train and bus tickets, so look back at those sections if you need more specific help during this process. You'll be given the option of paying for additional baggage, optional insurance, and get hit with taxes in the end, raising the ticket price.

- Now that you've booked your flight, make sure that you have your ticket confirmation and information in your email. You can print it out ahead of time or print it at the airport. Consider the conditions under which you're traveling—will you have an abundance of time when you get there? Will you be in a hurry?

Decide what you are doing to create your physical ticket, and make sure to bring an ID that matches your information. You may be able to check-in   using an app on your smartphone or QR code to save yourself from printing out a boarding pass.

- Arrive at the airport at least an hour and a half ahead of boarding time—and that could be pushing it. I try to arrive two hours early (and would suggest giving yourself much more, potentially several hours, for international flights). You never know if there will be long lines, slow security, or any complications. Sometimes, if you arrive "late", the check-in desk may not allow you to board the plane, even if there is technically still plenty of time. Those rascals! Use a few hours to go in early and save yourself the hassle of having to re-book tickets and losing several days in your plan!

- Get your ticket and check any bags if needed. Find your correct terminal, and head in that direction.

- You'll have to go through airport security. They'll ask you to remove your shoes, belt, jewelry, and other forms of metal. You'll have to send your personal items through a scanner, and they're very strict on what you can and cannot bring onto the plane. If you have supplements, liquids, or any other items that are limited or prohibited in a carry-on, make sure to put them in your checked luggage to be placed below the plane. Check all restrictions and size limits for liquids, etc., before heading to the airport.

- Once you find your terminal and double checked to make sure your information matches, you may have some time before your plane comes. This would be a good time to grab some plant-based food, stretch your legs, do headstands, take a power nap, listen to the Unruly podcast, or even read a book.

- While I'm flying, I like to talk to the people next to me if it feels like a nice fit, listen to music, watch movies, read, write, and daydream. Once you've had some experience flying, you'll get into your groove as well.

- When your plane lands, make sure you have all of your personal belongings. Exit the plane, and head to the place where you can collect your baggage. I like to make my luggage stand out! You can add stickers, bright ribbon or even something painted on your luggage so you can easily identify it when it comes down the conveyor belt at pickup.

If your flight is delayed or canceled, I have an awesome resource that can help you get money from the airline. I used Air Help for the first time this year and got $213.00 USD back for a flight being delayed! You can learn the specifics of how it works at **airhelp.com**. If you're going to use their services, please use the following link with the code "**unruly.**" I've signed up for a few affiliate programs for features and programs that I often use. Going through my link to file your claim will support me! The awesome part about this service is you can file claims from years back. Get online and give it a go!

Use my AirHelp link: *https://buff.ly/3doYNzd*

Safety tips for emotional and mental support while flying:
- Before flying, go over any anxieties you may have. How can you support yourself? How will you find your breath and calm if you feel your anxiety rising?
- Arrive at the airport early. Leave yourself enough time and space to go through the pre-flying process.
- Make sure you don't carry any items onto the plane that are prohibited. Security will stop you and there could be extra complications. If you're only going to be away from your checked bag(s) for a few hours or less, don't try to carry everything onto the plane. This can help you avoid trouble in the first place.
- Find your terminal and make sure you are there at boarding time with all of your personal items.
- After landing at your destination, make sure you collect all of your baggage.

Mantras:
- I arrive with ease and clarity to the airport. I effortlessly go through the pre-flying process, and board my plane, problem-free.
- The plane that I am on is protected by strong energies and gets me safely where I need to go.
- I am calm, present, and traveling with grace.

Resources:
- **Air Help:** File a claim to easily get money back on delayed or canceled flights from recent trips or years ago.

https://buff.ly/3doYNzd |
code: "unruly"

Get Creative!

I've given you more than a handful of ways to travel and offered specific insight/instructions on how you can participate in each. What works for you? At different points in your experience, you may want to consider playing with different modes of transportation. Meeting people on the go, traveling by train, and road-tripping are my personal favorites.

With all that being said, there are still 100 different ways I haven't listed in detail you could consider traveling by. Can you think of any? Just to warm your brain up, let me name a few. Have you considered going by longboard, sailboat, or on a cruise? Have you considered renting an RV, working for an airline to get free flights, or tagging along with your cousin's rowing team as they travel the USA to compete?

Think outside all of the boxes and bags. In a world full of ever-changing situations, weird opportunities, and people on the go, you're bound to find a way. I can't wait for you to add your new ideas and submissions to my next travel book tested and approved by you!

4

Places To Stay

"Every place is a goldmine. You have only
to give yourself time, sit in a teahouse
watching the passers-by, stand in a corner of
the market, go for a haircut. You pick up a
thread – a word, a meeting, a friend of a
friend of someone you have just met – and
soon the most insipid, most insignificant
place becomes a mirror of the world, a
window on life, a theatre of humanity."

— Tiziano Terzani

Places To Stay

As you're moving through the world in your travels, you'll most likely have to rest your body somewhere. In this chapter, we'll discuss some options for that. When we're designing our travel experience to work in a way in which money is not a large factor, we then come to the realization that paying for places to stay is a huge money-sucker.

Let's learn how to avoid this.

1. Couchsurfing

The first option (my personal favorite) is Couchsurfing. Yes, "randomly" finding someone's couch to stay on is an option we will

discuss later, but there is a potentially better and quicker way to stay in the homes of other folks.

What is Couchsurfing?
Well, I'm glad you asked. Great question! Couchsurfing is an app, and a website, that gives you access to a network of travelers offering their couches up around the globe. Not only is it cool to stay with other travelers in new places, but it comes at a very small fee that is well worth it. As of 2021, it costs $2.39 per month or $14.29 per year. (9) Hosts may

offer you a room in their house, a couch, sleeping bag, or a place to pitch a tent outside. Every host and house is different!

How does Couchsurfing work exactly?
I'll give you a general rundown of what Couchsurfing is, what it's like, and even how to get started. You'll understand so much better by actually playing with and using the app. Like I just mentioned, the Couchsurfing network is made up of travelers and like-minded humans around the globe. When you join Couchsurfing you set up a personal profile. On the profile, you're asked various questions about your personality, intentions, and life experiences. They always ask you about your wants and motivations behind joining Couchsurfing.

If you plan to offer up your space to others, they have a section for that on your profile as well. This section asks you specific details about your home, and encourages you to upload some photos, so others can see what your space is like. Being a host is a great way to score some good travel karma and help out a fellow traveler!

Once your profile is all set up, you can begin to use the app to look for places to stay. During or before travels, you can search a specific town, city, or area for open spaces, on specific dates. Next, you search and find someone who meets your needs. Send them a request to stay with them with a nice message. People on the Couchsurfing app do not have to get verified in any way, but they can choose to by applying for the mark of verification. When someone accepts your requested dates, you can message them to figure out further details.

Is it dangerous?
Just like anything else, Couchsurfing can be dangerous. You are putting yourself at risk by entering the home of someone that you don't know. But also remember they are possibly putting themselves at risk by letting a stranger – you – into their home.

I personally have always considered Couchsurfing a safe and very reliable option. I haven't had any terrifying experiences but I have had a couple uncomfortable ones. Overall, I would say with my experience and the experiences of others, it's a solid choice for those who are ready to test it out.

To make the process a little safer, the app lets you leave reviews for others. You can leave a personal review for people which is a general comment about them. It shows up on their profile. After you've stayed with someone, you rate them, mark various qualities that you felt matched them, and leave a review as well. They are not able to delete this review and they go through the same process for you.

So, what does this do for safety? It offers a way of gathering more information and ideas on folks before you stay with them. You get to read real comments left by other humans, comments that may contain warnings, stories, and positive feedback. I *always* check these first to learn more about my possible host!

How can I get started?
To get started, download the Couchsurfing app on your "smartphone", or go to **www.couchsurfing.com**. Let's discuss how to set up a profile online which will look very similar to setting up a profile through the app.

1. Once you're on the webpage, you'll be asked to enter your first name, last name, and email. Make sure that you have access to this email.
2. After this, it will ask you for your birthday, gender, and city where you exist.

3. Once you're in, click on "Edit My Profile." Here, you'll basically be advertising and presenting yourself. Once you get past the technical questions, you'll be taken to an "About Me" section. Add things you're passionate about here—cooking, reading sad novels, doodling, speaking Chinese, or rescuing ducks. Let people know what you're into. What do you want people to know about you?

4. You'll then be prompted to fill your "Why I'm on Couchsurfing" paragraph. Here, I encourage you to share your full intentions with Couchsurfing. What are you looking for when you arrive at their homes? What are you hoping to gain? To exchange? Be specific! People love knowing why you're here and what you're looking for. I often update this section, telling people about the trip that I'm currently on, and a few details on why I'm traveling at this moment.

5. After that, you get to fill out a section on your "Favorite Music, Movies & Books," "One Amazing Thing I've Done," and "What You Have to Teach, Learn, and Share." Answer these parts honestly, whatever that looks like to you. People want to know what you're all about and know what common interests you may share.

6. You'll then come to the "What I Can Share with Hosts" part. What can you share with your host? For me, I am always down to clean, help with projects, teach yoga, and share travel stories and tips. What do you have to offer? Be genuine. People usually aren't looking for much. They just want to share a new experience with another traveler.

7. After you have that all setup, you can add information and photos of your own home, if you're planning on letting folks surf at your house. Remember to update your "Accepting Guests" status whenever it changes.

8. Either way, make sure you upload some pictures of yourself to your profile. People love to consider what may happen with new experiences, and they'll probably be creating their own ideas of what you may be like when they're checking out your profile. Adding a face to the name and story helps.

9. If you want to get verified it's an extra charge. It is helpful but not required. I took the extra step to get verified because I use it

frequently and want to support the company. The benefits of this are that people will have more trust for you; Couchsurfing verifies your ID and address. You also get unlimited messaging and 24/7 support.

Alright, so now you have your profile. And you want to stay with someone. What do you do?

1. Login on the Couchsurfing app or website. Find the search bar where you are to enter your location. Type in the city or town name of where you intend to surf. If you're on the app, it'll only bring up possible hosts when you enter your destination. If you're on the computer, it'll bring up other options. Click "Find a Host."

2. For the next step, you'll be asked about your days of travel. When will you be arriving? When are you departing? Remember, these can always change. Try to stick to your dates, but sometimes things happen. Your host could cancel, you could cancel, or you could end up staying with them and ask to stay longer. You never know. Enter the number of travelers and hit "search." You have the option to add even more filters to your search, so feel free to explore with that option.

3. From there, you are able to scroll through lists of possible hosts. Check out the ones that say, "Accepting Guests." Whenever I am looking for a place to stay, I send out at least three requests. Couchsurfing is getting popular, and people are hosting more often. In big cities, people are used to getting multiple requests a day. When considering your options, make sure to check out their references and ratings. You want to make sure others have left this person great reviews and it sounds like they would be willing to stay with them again. Be cautious of folks who have little or no ratings. That makes it hard to learn anything about them. Read their full profiles because they often have special instructions for you to follow buried in the text when requesting to stay with them. They do this so they know you've spent time learning about them and you're making a conscious choice.

4. When you've found a possible host, send them a request. You'll have to enter your requested dates and number of travelers. You'll also be asked to attach a message explaining why you want to stay. Be honest, forward, and genuine. Why do you want to stay with them and what are you looking to get out of this interaction? What common interests do you share? Why do you think that you may bond well? Let them know.

5. When everything is complete, send out your message. You'll get a notification when they have either accepted or denied your request. If one person says no, don't give up. It only takes one to say yes.

6. When you've found a host, confirm your dates. Communicate to figure out their address, a way to contact them, and how + when you'll be getting to their home.

7. After Couchsurfing with a host, PLEASE leave an honest review! This lets other surfers know who—or what—may be waiting for them. Feel free to add how you felt around the person, any warnings, any fun memories, and exactly why you're leaving X number of stars. This helps keep other surfers safe. Expect them to leave you an honest review as well.

Food for the Brain

During one of my trips I met an incredible human being through Couchsurfing. Sam Hancock hosted me in Idaho Falls, Idaho. After working for a month, I was going to Idaho Falls to catch a break and meet up with a friend named Sara. I sent a request to stay with Sam for about six days. Compared to traditional Couchsurfing stays, this is a really long time! For some reason, Sam accepted my request. I chose to reach out to Sam because he looked pretty rad from his profile, and he had hosted over 100 people already. This offered a lot of reviews to look through, and I felt I had a good sense of what Sam might be like.

When I got to Sam's house, we were both tired and experiencing some emotions that felt draining. So, for the first couple of days we spent time in our rooms, coming out sometimes to eat or talk. Sam has an amazing setup for surfers by keeping his house comfy and in tip top condition.

I loved picking Sam's brain about his traveling adventures, experiences with Couchsurfing, his thoughts on mental illness and mental health, and about his existence so far. We had some of the best conversations and would often stay up until early in the morning with these exchanges.

As I was waiting for my friend Sara at Sam's house, her bus got canceled so her arrival time got pushed back. (Remember what I told you about the good ole' Greyhound buses?) With that happening, I asked Sam if I could stay at his house even longer. I ended up being there for over a week and it was honestly one of my favorite parts about my trip. I had no idea I would bond with and learn so much about Sam, or that I would so thoroughly enjoy his presence.

One night, we stayed up talking until about 5:00 AM. It was getting close to the arrival of my friend, bringing my departure closer, and we knew time was limited for the hike we were considering. We realized we only had the next day to conquer this hike if we really wanted to do it. We then woke up, on only a few hours of sleep, and laced up our hiking boots. Sleepy-eyed and barely awake, we made the two-hour drive to the Grand Tetons. I had no idea I was going to such an iconic and beautiful place and was pleasantly taken aback. After the hike, Sam posted a status and some photos about our trip saying,

"Taking my Couchsurfing guest and newest of friends on a hike to see the Tetons. We were running on less than four hours of sleep. But fueled with enthusiasm we finished the 7-mile hike (4,000 ft about half the height of climbing Mount St. Helens) just after sun-fall. Even though I've hiked this trail many times, experiencing it through the fresh eyes of Calen really made it spectacular all over again! Thank you for the adventure."

Although it was a long and challenging hike, we did it. Because of our late start, we ended up coming back down the mountain in the dark. I was honestly a bit terrified because I couldn't see the ground too well, was navigating through the pitch black, and knew that our circumstances increased the chance of being eaten by another animal. As the story goes, we made it, thankfully allowing me to write it all down today!

Eventually my friend came and Sam and I sadly parted ways. But don't worry, we came back and stayed with Sam again, after our trip to Yellowstone. I also did a week-long trip with Sam in Yosemite National Park years later. I just couldn't get enough of this wonderful soul. While staying with Sam I interviewed him for my podcast. This may be another one of my most favorite episodes so far, and you can find the link for it in the resources part of this section. If you want to get a good idea of what Couchsurfers/Couchsurfing is like be sure to check out this episode. Sam also gave out some great tips to stay safe for surfers and hosts alike.

Sam's interview is partly named *A Warm Bubble Bath for A Long Night*. Strange, right? During one of his first experiences with Couchsurfing, he ended up staying with someone who was intimidating, demanding, and Sam ended up being subtly forced into taking a bubble bath and trying on the clothes of a grown man. It's not graphically disturbing, but it is interesting, unsettling, and raw.

As I said, don't miss the article version of Sam's tips or the podcast episode! While we're Couchsurfing, we're putting ourselves in a position to be human and make real exchanges and memorable moments. This type of interaction is not your everyday experience, so enjoy soaking in all the benefits of Couchsurfing that you can!

Mantras:
- The universe always presents me with the best hosts. They are always considerate, respectful, and I am grateful for their presence.
- I always have a safe place to stay.
- I rest easy knowing that I am always protected, guided, and safe.

Resources:
- ***From One Couch to Another, How to CouchSurf During Travels (and stay safe):*** This resource is gold. When you check out the interview article and podcast episode from my blog, you'll get first-hand, (and very honest) information and insight from a pro. Article: *http://wanderwoman.online/index.php/2017/10/26/couchsurfing-sams-tips/*
Podcast Episode: *https://soundcloud.com/unrulystories/the-couchsurfing-king*

2. Tenting

Every time I leave my house prepared to travel on an extremely small budget, I always take a tent. It gives me the ease and security knowing I have some sort of shelter, no matter where I am.

To be completely honest, I'm not a fan of camping, especially alone, and especially in the dark. Although I love nature and have no problem with being without my traditional comfort items, camping doesn't usually appeal to me. Even so, you'll find a small tent strapped on my bike, or to my backpack. Other people love camping for so many awesome reasons!

If you are open to taking a tent with you, great. You don't even have to plan on using it, but knowing it is there may offer you some peace of mind. Some things that are awesome about tents is you can usually find them cheap, they can offer you a free place to stay, and you can set them up in many different settings. Consider a hammock in place of a tent if that speaks to you.

If you're working with a small budget, search on Craigslist, post on Facebook, and start asking around for a free tent. If you know that Uncle Jim cleans their garage out every summer and is an avid backpacker, this may be your time to shine.

I personally like taking a one-person tent because it's lighter and takes up less space. I can easily attach it to the bottom of my backpack and move it as needed. When you're looking for a tent, look for something that will be manageable. Once you physically have your tent, practice putting it up and taking it down a few times. This can offer the confidence and ease you need when working with your tent.

Now, I know what you may be asking:
Where will you set up your tent? Finding a spot to camp for the night can be a tricky deal, so let's explore some options. For additional ideas on where to set up your tent, please refer to the **Where to Stay** chapter where we discuss BLM (Bureau of Land Management) land and free camping apps and resources.

Biking Options

If you're biking, as we went over in the "biking" section of the book, the TransAmerica Trail maps will offer you different places to camp, and this can stay completely free. Some places may include actual campgrounds and local parks.

Campgrounds

This is a great option when looking for places to pitch your tent. They're built for this and often provide multiple amenities to campers. Some campgrounds cost money, so be aware of that when searching for some close to you. If you're looking for free ones, as I always am, get onto **Google** and search, "free campsites in __ location." Various resources and posts will show up, and you'll have to sort and sift through the information you're offered. Usually there are free camping spots, even if they're not in an official campground. You'll just have to figure out how to get to them.

Hipcamp

Hipcamp is another option that can be on the cheaper side. Go to hipcamp.com to book a spot at someone's house or property to tent camp, park an RV, stay in a cabin, sleep in a treehouse, or glamp.
Hot Tip: If you are set on camping, but can't find a free campground, call the one you wish to stay at and ask to work to pay off the fee. There is no guarantee that it'll work, but there are almost always extra chores to be done around campsites.

Yards

If you already know someone or know of some friends of friends in your area, but their house is full, ask to throw up your tent in the yard. This way you have a safe place to stay, a source of water and other resources, and people around you that you can reach out to.

Throw It Up

Not last night's beans and greens—your tent. Throw it up in a space that feels comfortable to you, a space that is not specifically designated for camping. This could be under a bridge, in an open field, or even on the side of the road. When doing this, be mindful of the humans that may be around, and if they will consider what you're doing as "trespassing" or if houseless people already occupy the space. We want to be mindful of personal bubbles. Some people can get really worked up so keep your safety in mind, especially if you are of marginalized experience that could put you in potentially dangerous situations. Check rules and regulations for the area.

Ask The Locals

There may be some ideal spots for putting up your tent you just don't see. This is where you ask the locals. You can talk to the local library or consider calling churches and asking to use some of their dirt to sleep on. In some parks, camping is allowed and supported, you just have to figure out which ones. When seeking advice don't share information with strangers about where you will be staying.

Although interacting with police officers is not suggested as a whole (especially for people of color, trans and queer individuals, or those with other marginalized identities), if you have the privilege to do so or just feel safe doing so, call and ask them where you can camp. It may help you know how to avoid them approaching your tent site later unexpectedly. If you are sharing tent space with others, be mindful of their safety, as well because their experience may present unique dangers and needs that do not immediately cross your mind, so practice social consciousness.

Food for the Brain

As I explained before, I'm not a huge fan of staying in a tent. If given options I would opt out of camping. But I have stayed in my tent, alone, more times than I can count. On one occasion I was on a bike tour and found a local park where camping was permitted. After I set up my tent, I used the small stream flowing through to wash my body and some clothes. I went dumpster diving and found some goodies, including ginger snap cookies.

While I was getting ready for bed that night, a man walked up to my tent. After talking to him for a bit, I understood that he was houseless, and that is where he stayed each night. I didn't get any bad vibes from him, but I was skeptical about being alone, in the dark, so close to another human. We talked a little bit longer over the recently salvaged gingersnaps. He seemed kind, gentle, and laid back. My anxiety still kicked up, though, when he told me they don't sleep at all during the night.

Trying to sleep that night was futile, I couldn't settle. I had so many fears and worries running through my head, and I kept imagining all of the bad things that could happen to me during the night with a stranger nearby. With my taser and mace close to me, I eventually fell asleep.

When I woke up the next morning, I was completely unharmed. The person I talked to the night before was still there and wide awake. We exchanged greetings as humans do in the morning and he told me there was a skunk hanging around the night before. He also informed me that the skunk was headed to my tent but he sent the critter in a different direction. As I started moving and walking around my tent, a faint smell of skunk spray lingered in the air, and I was grateful for the presence of another human.

Safety tips for tenting:
- Practice setting your tent up before you have to do it. It can be stressful if you're not familiar with how it works and you are trying to do it on a time schedule, in the dark, or in a new location.
- Carry some sort of light with you. It can be helpful for setting up your tent, watching your step, and looking for items in the dark.
- Be thoughtful about where you set up your tent. Is it on someone's property who may get upset? Is it far enough away from the road? Are you in a safe place?
- When asking for places to camp, don't tell strangers where you will be staying. Before you set up camp let someone that you trust know where your location is.

Mantras:

- My tent is a protected space keeping me safe from the elements and outside influences.
- I always find an ideal spot to pitch my tent.
- I easily find the perfect place to rest my body a night or whenever needed.

3. Meet Hosts (ATM)

Just as we discussed meeting people who could possibly help you get to your next destination at the moment (ATM) we'll do the same when in search of a place to stay. On some days, you

may meet some people you really connect with during your travels. These folks may offer you a couch to crash on, a bed, or some yard space to pitch a tent. Be open to new experiences— these could lead to new bonds and connections with others.

When talking to people throughout the day, mention you are traveling, and elaborate on how, and maybe why, you're doing it. People are often intrigued and wanting to help. This can provide the perfect opportunity for you to let them know your needs: a safe place to rest or stay.

Food for the Brain

Do you remember when we were talking about meeting people, ATM, and getting rides from them? I told a story about a person from a church who took me and my bike to my next destination. This person was on the way to a church camp, picking up kids along the way. On that very same day, I met the person who I now consider my adopted Grandpa.

The story goes as such: After the person driving the kids and I reached a certain point, before church camp, they dropped me off in a small, cozy town, along the coast of California. I knew nothing about the town or area at the time, but I was in what's known as the Emerald Triangle.

When I bring that name up now, people often talk about how magical the area is and how much love they have for it. When I got dropped off in an unknown town, in a grocery store parking lot, I had no idea where I would be staying for the night and evening was approaching fast. I felt a little bit of panic prickle up inside of me but decided not to indulge it. It sounds like something from a movie, but my intuition told me that it would be okay if I just walked to the doors of the supermarket. So, I did.

Before I could even reach the door, I saw some curious characters. I distinctly remember seeing four people: one wearing a suit with crystals attached to it, who had a live parrot sitting on their shoulder; another person, who was masculine-presenting, with a strong build, and long, dark, flowing curly hair; a third person, who was older, with a white beard and a kind smile; and the final person, who was a beautiful woman, with warm and glowing energy.

As I was walking into the store the one with curly hair asked me about my bike. It turned out that they liked to bike too, and they were really interested in my trip and travels. They then asked me where I was staying for the night, and I expressed my concern about having no idea.

They immediately offered me a place to stay at their house as long as I could get my bike up the huge hill that acted as their driveway. They then turned to the older fellow next to them and introduced me to the person known to the town as "Brother Tom." After talking to Brother Tom for a few seconds, he also offered me a place to stay. After chatting with them, we decided it would be easier for me to stay with Tom, because he lived only about a mile away, and there was no hill in front of his house to climb.

Before we wrapped up our conversation I wandered into the store, and the woman assured me these people were good; she had been traveling and met the bunch when she got to town. She had been staying and hanging with this crew for a couple of weeks and trusted them.

After getting some groceries I met Brother Tom in the cafeteria section. I then followed him to his house, leading me via bike. Tom had a roommate who agreed I could stay for the night. They offered me my own room in their house with a mattress and a space to bring in my bike.

Over the next couple days, Tom really started to feel like family to me. We went and explored the town together: woodshops, cafes, and the downtown area. We took a road trip to see the redwood trees and Tom told me about his days as a hitchhiker, giving me some of the tips that are now included in this book!

When we made it to the redwoods, Tom and I rode our bikes together for miles and miles. To my surprise, I struggled a bit to keep up with Tom, who is almost in his 70s. After a day of riding, eating packed salads, and receiving advice on dealing with men, we headed back for the house. When the sun was setting, we pulled over to a beach and Tom read a passage out of one of his favorite books to me.

Although it sounds strange to some, I now honestly can say you can truly have friends and loved ones of all ages. Most of us have one thing in common: we want to provide care and be cared for. That night, when we got back to the house, Tom finished a story out of the book that he was reading to me and tucked me in as I fell asleep. People: this is no joke. I had such a beautiful time with someone that I had never planned to meet, a situation that started out with fear of the unknown. I ended up staying with Tom for days and it felt really hard to  leave. We still keep up with each other and send emails and snail mail back and forth every so often. This may not happen to you every single time you are lost and looking for a place to stay, but this is a great example of that travel magic.

Safety tips for meeting people "ATM" and staying with them:

- Don't tell anyone your exact travel plans, or needs, while figuring out if they are the right fit for you. If you change your mind, you don't want them to know exactly where you will be and what you will be doing.

- If you have a bad feeling about a situation while planning, don't follow through.
- If you have bad feelings while in a situation, leave in the safest way possible.
- Always let someone know who you are staying with and the exact address.
- Tell whoever you are staying with you have shared this information.

Mantras:
- Every space that I enter holds safety and comfort for me.
- I easily create my travel experiences.
- Every human that I meet has the best intentions, that honor me, for our time together.

4. Hostels

Let me just come right out and say it: Hostels are awesome. They can be super cheap, offer really cool spaces, and are usually full of other travelers. If you plan to travel often it's a good idea to familiarize yourself with these spaces.

What is a hostel?

A hostel is a community space where people pay for a shared place to rest. Some hostels are free, but I've only come across one of these in my travel life so far. If you want to get a feel of what hostels are like, imagine a big house or building that has individual rooms, a community hangout space, a front desk, a community kitchen, and often some sort of outdoor space.

They can be very different; one hostel I went to was set up in a garage, on a farm, and guests slept inside on cots, outside in hammocks, or in the hay with the chickens. Other hostels are a bit more decorated and have large bathroom spaces, fresh towels, and themed rooms. Inside of the individual rooms of hostels there are different choices for sleeping. You can pay more for a private room, pay the least amount to occupy a bunk bed in a room full of other random people, or sometimes you can choose to be in an "all female" room for added safety.

Just how expensive are hostels?

Hostels in the USA usually range from $15.00 to $24.00 a night for a space in a shared room. But as I said, nothing is set in stone and prices vary by country. If you're looking to stay for free, call, email or ask the hostel in person if you can do some work for an exchange. Some hostels already have exchange programs set up and may even ask you to stay longer while offering you work there. They're usually pretty open to exchanges like this!

What is the atmosphere like?
Hostels are some of my favorite places because they are usually made up of extremely different and interesting people from all over the world. Most people staying in hostels are bikers, backpackers, wanderers, and travelers. You can often find people hanging out, reading books, trading jokes, cooking meals together, partying, and getting some online time in hostel spaces. Hostels are geared towards travelers so they're equipped to help you with your traveler-needs. They know the hottest local hangouts, the cheapest restaurants, the best adventure companies, and usually have people working that speak various languages.

- To find a hostel near you, go to **hostelworld.com**. Please use my affiliate link below in the resource section! You can then check out the local hostels and compare what they have to offer, along with their prices.
- Booking a hostel room is very similar to booking a hotel room and you can do all of the work online. All booking sites are different and should offer clear instructions on how to book your stay with them.
- When staying in a hostel, be mindful of the others in the area. Wash your dishes, clean up your trash, and be open to sharing.
- Keep your valuables locked up or close to you and make sure that you feel safe in the room that you are assigned. If something or someone feels off, request a room change.

I can't name one place that is 100% safe, and unfortunately, hostels are no exception. I've heard stories from different people who have experienced sexual harassment and other potentially dangerous situations. For the full interview, and tips to stay safe, check out the podcast interview with Divina, an incredible person that I met and immediately felt connected with in a hostel in Las Vegas.

To paint a picture for you of what the hostel experience may be like, we recorded a podcast episode together after only a few hours of knowing each other. Before this, we started talking by sharing our stories of travel, sexual harassment, and technical route plans and adventures for the near future. We then went on a hunt for plant-based ice cream to fight the Las Vegas heat, and then retreated, settling in the living space to share a couch and watch *Moana* with others. It was a full, well-rounded, tasty, and solid day.

Food for the Brain

As you can see, hostel spaces are super unique and can be super fun. Some of them have outdoor pools and most of them have libraries where you can trade in your used book for another's. If hostels were free, I would split my time between them and Couchsurfing. I've always left hostels with a good taste in my mouth, and I've always found people there with whom I'm more than happy to give my time.

While backpacking through South America, my travel family and I, made up of exchange students, would stay in hostels along the way. Doing so gave us an opportunity to rest, get information about our location from the locals, and have some fun. They also provided us with a space to hang out together, get some alone time, or choose to engage with others that were staying in the hostel as well.

Hostels, to me, represent sharing. Someone is sharing a homey space with you, a cultural exchange, and you also have the option of sharing with others from all around the world. Some of my favorite things I have shared in hostels are plant-based meals, books, cultural exchanges through conversation, tips, information about places I've been that is helpful to others, and memories with my travel family.

Safety tips for staying in hostels:
- Keep your valuables locked up, close to you/with you at all times. Bring your own lock or rent one from the hostel.
- If you do go out partying with others from the hostel and take any substances make sure that you are in control of yourself or

have someone to look out for you, have a way to communicate with others, and have a plan to get back to the hostel.
- If you feel uncomfortable in the room you're assigned request a room change.
- Let someone trusted know what hostel you're staying at and how long you plan to be there.

Mantras:
- I easily meet and connect with others who help me along my way.
- I am open to accepting new opportunities for adventure, exchange, and valuable connection into my life.

Resources:
- ***#6 He Made You Pasta, And Then Forced You to Kiss Him?! Pt. 1, Sexual Harassment***: **CW: Sexual assault.** This resource is the podcast episode that was created with the person, mentioned above, that I met in a Las Vegas hostel. This episode is not to scare you but to offer insight as to what travel experiences can really be like. In this episode, we also touch on queerness and other travel topics.
  https://soundcloud.com/unrulystories/hostels-and-sexualassult
- ***Hostel World***: Go to the site to book through this link to help support me, my projects, and future travels:
  https://buff.ly/3e1SMHG

5. BLM Land and Searching for Free Camping Spots

During this most recent cross-country road trip in 2021 I discovered more tips and tricks to add to this chapter. Have you heard of BLM (Bureau of Land Management) land before? They state on their website that their mission is to "sustain the health, diversity, and productivity of public lands for the use and enjoyment of present and future generations." (10) Basically, they allow people to stay on specific land for free. Across the USA you can find places to tent camp, park a vehicle, motorhome or RV, and set up shop for a while. There are some folks who permanently drift from one BLM site to another, and those who stay put in one spot for as long as possible. The best way to figure out if there is BLM land near you is to go to the website, www.blm.gov, or call and ask the closest National Park.

BLM land is also found easily through free parking/camping apps such as Park4Night and freecampsites.net, which brings me to my next point. Both resources allow users to go on to the app or website and mark sweet (or not so sweet) camping and parking spots that they've found throughout the country. After the managers approve a new camping/parking location, people can see the exact address and coordinates of each spot, as well as real reviews and photos. If you use either of these resources, please rate and review each spot that you visit! It helps other wanderers understand exactly what they are getting into when sleeping in a listed area for the first time.

You may come across some marked locations on the apps that are not technically legal to park in. Everyone has to decide what risks they are willing to take, but we found that when it comes to parking in a van, RV, or motorhome for the night, there is strength in numbers. We noticed that we were able to stay at "illegal" parking spots easier when there were a lot of other folks parked there too. We also always had some sort of story prepared as to why we couldn't drive anymore and had to pull over and park in said spot. If you have the unfortunate experience of coming in contact with police, consider telling them that you got too tired to drive and didn't want to put anyone else on the road in danger.

6. More "Traditional" And Generic Travel Spaces

We're not going to go too deep in this section—but there are a few more options when looking for places to stay. They are usually more expensive, and some of them have a more formal feel to them.

Hotels, motels, and inns fall under this category. They are usually the most expensive places to stay in and don't offer the same type of community and travel atmosphere as the other options I talked about previously. If you're really set on staying in one of these spaces, you can choose to pay for it or use the methods in **chapter six** to ask to work in exchange for a place to stay. I've personally never done this, but as you know, it's worth trying!

There is one more idea that I'd like to mention, and that is spaces provided through Airbnb. If you go to **www.airbnb.com**, you can create a profile and begin searching for places to stay. The way that Airbnb works is that you rent out a room, or the entire space, in someone else's home.

I've used this company so many times to book a room, or house, depending on my budget at the time. These settings have a different feel to them! It's a mix of being a guest at someone's house, but still having personal space, all while feeling like you're staying at a hotel. Hosts will often offer you fresh towels, treats, and other items that could improve your experience. If you're looking for more information on Airbnb, check out their website to cruise through more details. Check out my most favorite Airbnb find of all time as of 2021 in the resources below!

In Summary

These are not the only spaces that exist for you and other travelers. A great resource to use for finding a place to stay is the Worldwide Opportunities on Organic Farms (**WWOOF**) site. While WWOOFing, you work on an organic farm in exchange for food and a place to stay. This is one of the main networks that I use during my travels because it covers so many needs and helps you meet other like-minded folks. In **chapter six** we'll go over exactly how to do this in more detail.

What I want you to really, *really*, understand is this: Where you choose to stay has a huge influence on your trip. It will change your energy and can take you into a whole other head and heart space.

Just because you once committed to staying somewhere, or with someone, doesn't mean that you have to follow through. I hope you are always able to exit situations that are undesirable or have turned dangerous as quickly as possible. However, I do recognize not everyone has the privilege of safely entering and/or leaving spaces at all times. If you do end up finding yourself in a position that is potentially dangerous or harmful to you, please refer to the hotlines at the end of the book.

Because this guide is more informational than anything, I really haven't come right out and shared with you why I truly love travel. Part of it is the exchange with new places and the earth around me, but most of it is the connections that I make with people. When you're locating and choosing places to stay, look for places that have the most of this to offer to you. That's where you'll grow, rest, thrive, and feel whole again.

5

Finding Food

"The common sense rules
of the 'real world'
are a fragile collection
of socially reinforced illusions."

- Timothy Ferriss

Finding Food

If you want to keep moving, it is recommended that you consume some calories. But before we talk about food, I want to define what food means to me, and how I like to use it. If you look at the "typical" diet in the USA, it consists of dead bodies (flesh from animals), stolen animal secretions (such as dairy and eggs), and highly processed food. I have my fair share of processed foods, but I do not consume anyone else's flesh or things taken from their bodies. My diet is plant-based and it fits into my vegan lifestyle and liberationist, social justice philosophy.

There are numerous reasons as to why you should not be eating someone else's dead body, or the "products" they suffered to create, but we could be here for hours with this discussion. So, in the resources below, I'll leave you some material to fork through as to why you should work to divest from participating in the cruelty against other animals, your body, the environment, and the well-being of the world.

I would like to add during multiple trips across the USA, and traveling five continents, I've not once been left optionless for food or stepped outside of a plant-based diet on purpose. Once you learn how to eat plant-based, by replacing the products that you're already consuming with their plant-based alternatives or finding that nutrition elsewhere, you get into a groove that makes it almost effortless and enjoyable.

I understand we all have different bodies that react to foods in a multitude of ways, but if it's not plant-based, I don't consider it food.

Period, end of story (unless you have well thought through questions and would like to start a meaningful discussion on the topic, then I'm all ears and heart).

I also understand food scarcity is real, especially for those living in poverty and/or those who are unsheltered; both issues that predominantly affect Black folks, Indigenous folks, People of Color, and those in the LGBTQ+ community, among others.

If you look at the ways in which a lot of humans in the USA get food, by grocery shopping or going out to eat, you may notice it gets costly. Food is not cheap and "higher quality food" can get really expensive. As we discussed in the last two chapters, we've eliminated or found ways around two huge costs: transportation and having a place to stay. In this section, we're about to tackle another big one.

1. Buying Food

This option is simple and straight to the point. The first option you have is buying your food along the way. Although I treat myself sometimes at restaurants when I have the cash, I try to avoid eating out. One meal could easily turn into $20, which could have supplied you with home-cooked meals for two to three days.

That leaves us buying our food from the grocery store. You can come up with money in multiple ways: by being already prepared with money or making it on the road, or by using the techniques that we describe in **chapter six.**

When grocery shopping, look for items that are plant-based, nutritional, provide you with the energy that you need, and meet the needs of your taste buds. If you know about and practice Ayurveda, you can keep these principals around food in mind while shopping. Buy (mostly) items that won't spoil easily, unless you have constant access to a fridge. Try to buy things in bulk from the bins because this will save you money and cut down on waste.

Here are some things to consider when choosing what to eat while traveling:

Nutrition: It can be easy to mindlessly grab a cheap can of soup and chow down. Let me tell you, I've done it a countless number of times! A can of Progresso lentil soup used to be my go-to after a long day.

There's no shame there but be sure to plan out some healthier meals that are more nutrient dense as well, especially if your trip involves being active.

Weight & Space: Consider how much room you have to carry food, how much you can physically manage, and what foods will be most compact and easily carried. This is especially important for those who are hiking or backpacking.

Durability: Be mindful of foods that are susceptible to spilling, getting bruised, or mashed up easily during travel.

Cost: If you're on a tight budget then it's a good idea to stay away from convenience store food and restaurants. Have a solid list of meals you're excited to prepare and consume.

Ease Of Preparation: You may find yourself traveling with a minimal amount of cookware. Look for meals that are quick and easy to prepare while out and about.

Taste & Variety: If you plan on traveling for an extended period of time, consider having many yummy recipes and options up your sleeve to keep you from burning out on the same few foods.

Environmental and Ethical Issues: It is important to always consider how our choices affect the planet, humans, and other nonhuman animals when engaging in consumerism. However, sometimes it feels hard to put our values into action considering the consumerist world we live in. Too often we are unaware of the atrocious acts committed to create the products we purchase. I encourage all of you to never stop learning, keep an open and inquisitive mind, a watchful eye, and try to consume in the most loving way you know how.

Hot Tip: A great way to practice for your trip is to put your cookstove and other cooking devices that you will be using while traveling in your kitchen at home. Also add whatever cookware you might bring with you. Before you leave, try out different recipes and combinations of food that will be available to you on the road. Get creative and come up with some meal ideas on your own or search the internet for some fresh ideas. Try out some of the recipes listed below. Practicing at home will help you walk into your eating and cooking time while traveling with more confidence and will likely help you save money!

Let's look at an example of what my daily food intake looks like while traveling for some yummy inspiration:

Breakfast Ideas:
- Peanut butter and banana sandwich
- Avocado toast with nooch, garlic salt and possibly veggies
- Bagels with one of the following spreads: hummus, vegan cream cheese, avocado or guacamole, any nut butter and jelly. You can also go for savory toppings like lettuce, tomato, sprouts, cilantro, nutritional yeast, garlic powder, and Tofurkey slices. Consider these sweet toppings: bananas, apples, maple syrup, cinnamon, nutmeg.

Burrito Love:
- Burritos can be appreciated at any time of day.
- Rice and beans are key. Get fast-cooking rice that comes in a bag for an easier and cheaper experience that also saves on fuel!
- Canned pinto and black beans are delicious in burritos. They can sometimes be too heavy and bulky to carry around when backpacking. Consider taking beans in a bag or dehydrated refried beans, which can sometimes be found in the bulk section of co-ops, when backpacking.
- Zucchini and squash can be an excellent filling choice for burritos. They are cheap to buy and easy to prepare. They also don't bruise as easily as other vegetables.
- Try adding mushrooms, peppers, broccoli, onions, and garlic to your burritos!
- You can also add cucumbers, tomatoes, avocado, cilantro, greens, hot sauce, or salsa.
- You can take all of the ingredients mentioned above, minus the tortilla, to make a bomb Southwest breakfast bowl.

- Rice bowls are also good to pile on all the veggies you love and top with your favorite toppings.
- Depending on how you are traveling, a lot of the ingredients can be prepared prior to your trip and stored in containers.

Consider Ramen:

- While on our van trip across the USA in 2021 we ate a lot of ramen because it was quick and easy to prepare and very cheap to purchase.
- Add any of the following to boiling water: yellow squash, zucchini, mushrooms, or broccoli.
- Add ramen shortly after.
- The vegetables should be ready around the same time as the ramen. Drain the water to your liking and stir in the ramen packet.
- Munch and enjoy!

Deck Out Your Oatmeal:

- Oatmeal is almost always a winner. Even if you don't have any way to heat it, it's something filling and versatile.
- You can jazz it up by pairing it with some additions like fruits, nuts, seeds, nut butters, and syrups.
- Get instant oats and let them soak in water for a few minutes. After they are ready, deck your bowl out and dig in.

Awesome Vegetables to Have on Hand:

- Zucchini and squash: These two veggies are cheap, easy to cook, and are harder to bruise. Great for backpacking.
- Mushrooms, avocado, onion, garlic, broccoli, spinach, salad greens

Get Condiments Free from Supermarkets:

- Hot sauce packets, ketchup, mustard, relish, salt, and pepper from their food bars or food prep stations

Spice Mixes to Make Ahead of Time:
- Thai curry spice mix
- Chili spice mix
- Brown sugar and cinnamon + other spices for oatmeal (Could add nuts and hemp seeds, chia seeds, flax etc.)

Other Meal Ideas:
- Chickpea salad sandwich
- Coconut curry
- Chili
- Pancakes
- Fruit leathers
- Peanut chickpea curry
- Vegan banana bread
- Energy balls
- Trail mix
- Dried fruit

When I hit the grocery store and find these items, I can easily eat for less than $10 a day. Keep track of what you're spending and how many days it lasts you. It is unique for all of us because we all have different needs, but I've found it's not hard to find things that nurture my body and keep cash in my bag as well.

As you can see, there are a variety of affordable plant-based foods that can be found in most grocery stores. You can mix and match what you eat at different times and add to the shopping list I use. You know what you like, so come up with your own. How much you buy depends on where you're going, what you're able to carry, and when you'll have access to food next.

2. Work in Direct Exchange for Food

On my first travel adventure across the USA, I decided to try to work for the things I wanted. If I was hungry, I would stop in a local restaurant and ask to work for food for the day. Before starting that trip, my biggest fear was my plan wouldn't work.

I also must acknowledge my privilege here. I've never gone hungry. I know others experience food insecurity due to capitalism, classism, racism, and other structures such as these. With such an abundance of plants on Earth, everyone could (and should) be well fed.

That's a larger conversation to keep exploring at another time! If you want to learn more on your own, check out the organizations shared in the resources below.

During my trip, I found some nontraditional ways to eat. I would save up money for food, have food given to me, dumpster dive, or work in direct exchange for it.

After thinking about some of the reactions I've received when telling people I ask to work for food, I think some people feel silly, or even embarrassed, when considering this as an option. It may have something to do with the fact we feel like we "can't provide" for ourselves in a way that society says is normal and right, or we often think we're above doing jobs like these. If your first reaction is to pull away from this option, simply ask yourself why that is. Another common misconception people may cling on to after hearing my stories is this is a seamless plan that works for everyone. That's not true! Many unhoused people are unable to find work or are instantly rejected when trying this.

Working for food this way has some pros and cons. The pros are you don't have to work ahead of time and save up, and also, you meet people and build relationships through asking and working. Another possible pro, depending on your intention, maybe it typically pushes you out of your comfort zone. The main con is people aren't always open to exchange food for your work, and you may find yourself feeling panicked if you don't have a backup option.

Sometimes people say "no," and that's okay. Remember, you are asking for something directly, and people can choose how they want to respond. Some people will want to give you work but don't have the power in that situation to do so. Some people will say they don't need the extra help. Some people will be confused, and it will take them a moment to make up their minds, and that is also okay. The most important thing is you ask in the first place.

How do you ask? Let's talk this through. First, I'll provide you with my own example of what I've used when asking to work for food:

"Hello, my name is Calen Otto. I'm currently traveling by bike across the United States, to see new things, and make new connections. I'm also doing it on an extremely small budget and working for things I need along the way. I'm looking to work in direct exchange for a meal, is that a possibility here?"

Let's break it down a little.

- First, introduce yourself. State your name, and what you are currently doing, and why. Here, we're just looking to explain your current experience to others. I often find that people are not only interested in travel, but also like to know your motivations behind it. If you can offer them something new and honest, they're more likely to pay attention.
- Second, let them know you're doing it with little money. If they understand this, then they can see why it's important for you to be asking this question, and also find opportunities to meet your needs.
- Lastly, let them know why you're here, speaking to them. What do you need? Ask for it. Let them know up front what you are good at and what kind of experience you have.

Even though I personally don't believe we should have to work hard for basic needs, like shelter and food, the ruling class seems to disagree and has most parts of society set up accordingly.

Some jobs restaurants may give you can include:
- Sweeping or mopping
- Cleaning prep areas
- Cleaning outside structures
- Smashing boxes or moving trash
- Handling and preparing food items

Restaurants are not the only places that are possibilities for work. Check grocery stores, small businesses, and farmer's markets.

Food for the Brain

The first time I ever asked to work for food was on my first day of bike touring. I had just completed 67 miles and was beat. I was planning to stay at a church for the night and came across a small grocery store/food vendor a couple of miles beforehand. While I had planned to live off Clif bars and whatever the church gave me to eat, seeing all of the food made me feel like I wanted to act otherwise.

I was so nervous to ask for work I was practically shaking. When I approached the counter, I spat up the same words you looked over in the example sentence. The person behind the counter stayed calm, cool, and was open to listening. They immediately said yes—and told me I wouldn't have to be doing any sort of work. It turned out they were the owners of the store, and they were genuinely interested in supporting me. They pulled out a shopping bag, and had me follow them around, pointing out things I liked.

To add onto that, they had me follow them over to the café area and point out what sandwich I wanted from the menu. I was shocked. At that moment, I felt my heart defrost a little, and some of my fears around rejection melt away.

While the owner was preparing the food, they encouraged me to sit down and rest outside, so I did. I started talking to another person who was also relaxing outside, who turned out to be their partner. We had such a wonderful conversation, one I was not expecting, but instantly made space for.

I was so shocked by how much kindness these folks showed me. I decided to turn that energy into gratitude and express it in the best way I could manage. After I felt full, not only of food, but also meaningful conversation, they sent me on my way, leaving me with their phone numbers. I assured them if I had any problems I would call as requested. I can't remember the names or faces of these people, but I will *truly* always remember how they encouraged me to feel that day and the energy they sent with me.

On one occasion, I walked into a chain pizza shop and asked if I could work for some food. The person behind the counter looked straight confused for about thirty seconds, but then handed me a tiny broom and told me that the parking lot needed to be swept. As I was outside, sweeping, with the world's tiniest broom, I couldn't help but laugh. I was sweating, with the sun beating down on me, as I slowly picked the dirt up off of the ground outside. The job didn't really make sense to me.

Before I had finished, one of the workers came outside and told me that it was enough. I followed them back inside, where they let me know I could help myself to anything on the pizza and salad bar. While I was eating, the server kept coming back to ask me more about my travels. I had so many emotions going at that moment and realized the world is a strange place. I had just picked dirt and trash off the dirty ground in exchange for pizza. In these moments, you often realize things don't have to make sense to feel right.

Hold on, I have one last occurrence to share with you. During a bus layover, I found myself in Salt Lake City, UT. I had a few hours before I would catch my next bus and was starting to get hungry. After an hour or so of wandering around, I came across a farmer's market. I was so delighted because I heard these were good spots to find work exchanges. So, I walked right up to a booth with confidence, and expressed what I was doing, and my needs.

The person behind the table turned angry. He told me he was tired of people asking to do this and that it didn't make sense. That I should be paying for things with real money. I instantly felt discouraged.

Thoughts of not being worthy enough, feeling discouraged and unwanted, washed through me. With that wave of emotions I abandoned the farmer's market. As I was walking back to the bus station, tired and upset, I saw a sign that looked like nothing but pure

magic to me. It read "Raw Vegan Organic Food." If I had to pick a favorite type of food group at the time, it would be just that. I instantly pulled my head up and my legs took me inside.

As soon as I opened the doors, I realized that this place meant serious business. The food looked fresh and well thought through. The restaurant was clean and beautiful. I awkwardly approached the hostess and explained what I was doing. At first, she told me no. Not in a harsh way, but very gently. She also explained you had to be 21 to enter the restaurant, and I was 19 at the time. I can't remember how I responded, but she reconsidered, and formulated a plan.

She took me outside with a bag and told me it was my job to pull the weeds and clean the place up. I was thrilled! I had never been so eager to rip plants out of the ground in my whole life. When I was finished, she brought me back inside and sat me down at the booth. She then fully took care of me. She asked me what I wanted, with no restrictions, and even encouraged me to order an expensive raw dessert. When she had time, she would come sit down and talk to me. I enjoyed her presence so much and didn't realize my body had been craving intention, care, and soft energy for a while.

We talked about my life, her life, and all of the in-between. Before I left, she took my picture, shared my story on her social media, and thanked me. *Thanked me!* Thanked me!?! We both gained so much from our short and sudden interaction that I emotionally didn't want to leave. To this day, I still admire this person, and am thankful for the exchange of gratitude and honesty we made.

Safety tips for protecting your energies and emotions when looking for work:
- Ask directly for what you need.
- Don't apologize for doing things in a non-traditional way.
- Remember individuals may say "no," but that is not always the final or only answer.
- If you don't feel safe or aligned in doing work that is asked of you, turn it down.

Mantras:
- I always have enough calories, the right nutrition, and food my body needs.
- I nourish my body easily and fully.
- I always have what I need, in each new moment.

3. Dumpster Diving

Have you ever dived into a dumpster? I haven't either. But I have stepped into dumpsters in search of food. You'd be surprised what you can find. Some folks make this an everyday event and skip the line in the grocery store. Grocery stores are quick to throw out bruised or "ugly" produce, something that has "expired" or something that doesn't look right. A large portion of our society in the USA is very wasteful. On this occasion, our wastefulness may score you some free meals.

Won't I get sick? As with everything else that we've talked about in this book, there is some type of risk involved. You could get sick. I know a lot of folks who do this and have read many blogs and articles about dumpster diving. Each person has reported never getting sick and I personally haven't gotten sick from dumpster diving, either.

The pro to dumpster diving is you can find some really great food, and it's all free. The con is that you have to search for it and do so without getting in trouble.

The risk for dumpster diving changes from place to place and with different privileges. Find out about the regulations around dumpster diving where you're at before you do it so that you have a chance to consider your options. I've never been seen, or even spoken to, when dumpster diving. There are other folks who have reported being asked to leave.

If you do get arrested for dumpster diving, or fined, you can get your ticket paid for. Rob Greenfield, environmentalist and activist, promises to pay for it and does.

Check out more details at this link:
http://robgreenfield.tv/arrestedfordumpsterdiving/

Rob says, "Here's the deal:

If you get arrested or ticketed for dumpster diving for food, I promise to pay the ticket(s), get media coverage to the issue, and make sure you are in safe hands. I will even travel to your town to be there in person if it will add to the positive impact of the event. This promise is good for the USA and Canada but if you are in another country and in need of help, please contact me and I'll see if I can lend a hand." (11)

As dumpster diving is getting more popular, grocery stores and businesses are cracking down a little more with security measures like locks, fences, and cameras. Not only do I see active travelers doing it, but people who are more settled and are choosing not to pay for groceries are participating as well.

I have found that many fences can be opened easily, many locks are not really closed, and my presence usually goes unnoticed. I think as people realize there isn't any real harm in dumpster diving (other than society's imposed rules and prejudices), it's becoming more and more accepted. Dumpster diving without trouble is still a privilege itself because so many homeless people are seen as a "problem" for doing this, as well as "dirty" and "gross."

- When you're ready to dumpster dive, find a local grocery store, market, or restaurant that has dumpsters accessible. Take some sort of carrier with you. Once you have the dumpster open, you either have to reach inside—or my favorite—climb in.
- Sort through the food, as much as you feel comfortable, looking for items that you'd like to consume. You never know what you're going to find!
- When you're done, make sure that you don't leave a mess. If you do they could start locking the dumpster, making it inaccessible for others who may be into diving as well, or for those who rely on this method to obtain their only food for the day.
- If something doesn't smell, taste, or look right to you, don't finish eating it. Trust your body and its senses.

You may be surprised at how many salvageable things you'll encounter in dumpsters. I've found fresh produce, packaged treats, bakery-made bread, and more. If you have extra food, consider sharing with others. In the resources section below I'll share some really helpful articles and media from Rob Greenfield about dumpster diving and the bigger idea behind it.

In Summary

Now that I've shared my three main ways that I collect food with you, it's time to wrap this chapter up. But first, I want to mention that these aren't the only ways:

You'll have to think through this one yourself, but if you qualify, you may want to consider using food stamps. I currently have conflicting feelings about this (for me personally) because I want to be outside of the system, but I also don't mind using its resources. This isn't a debate, but something for you to consider. The process can move slowly, but when it finally comes through, it's nice to have extra support.

Another great resource to use to find food is **WWOOFing**. As we talked about before, it's a website that connects you with organic farms and they ideally provide food for you. In the next chapter, we'll talk about how to WWOOF.

When you're on the road, you're likely to run into other travelers who are willing and ready to share food. Take it, if it's desirable to you, and give when you can. You'll probably notice the repeated theme of sharing so don't be afraid to dive in!

Speaking of taking food, have you read *Steal This Book* by Abbie Hoffman yet? He has thought up other ways to get food for little or no money!

Resources:

- *10 Tips for Dumpster Diving Success*: This resource is an article by activist Rob Greenfield. It provides some awesome insight as to how to successfully dumpster dive. *http://robgreenfield.tv/dumpsterdivingtips/*
- *Arrested for Dumpster Diving for Food? I've Got You Covered*: Here you can find more information on Rob's promise to help, if you run into any trouble dumpster diving. *http://robgreenfield.tv/arrestedfordumpsterdiving/*
- *Food Waste Activism and Dumpster Diving Resource Guide*: With this article, you can learn how to be a part of the solution to the food waste problem. *https://www.robgreenfield.org/foodwasteguide/*
- *Eating Plant-Based On A Budget*: This is a resource that I created to give suggestions on cheaper and alternative ways to find food. *http://wanderwoman.online/index.php/2018/07/22/eating-plant-based-on-a-budget/*
- *Why Travellers Shouldn't Be Consuming Flesh Or Stolen Animal Secretions*: Learn my ethics behind living vegan and the rejection of eating animal bodies and secretions.

http://wanderwoman.online/index.php/2017/07/27/travelequal svegan/

- **How To Navigate "Traditional" Menus While Traveling As Vegan**: I wrote this guide to help you navigate normal menus as someone who eats their ethics after living in Chile, in a meat-heavy culture for a year.
  http://wanderwoman.online/index.php/2017/05/01/eat-well-and-travel-vegan/

- **Influencers: Stop Sharing Photos Of Your Fishing Trips And Fish Dinners. The Ocean Is Dying. (And This Is Partly Why)**: Learn the facts that you should know before eating fish bodies.
  http://wanderwoman.online/index.php/2020/09/18/stop-fishing/

- **Free From Harm**: This is an incredible non-profit based in Chicago dedicated to building a nonviolent mass movement of liberation for all species. They share awesome free resources on why and how to live a vegan life.
  https://freefromharm.org

- **Food Empowerment Project**: Their goal is to create a "more just and sustainable world by recognizing the power of one's food choices".
  https://foodispower.org

- **A Well-Fed World**: They believe that "A global shift towards plant-based foods more efficiently uses crops and natural resources to alleviate hunger, increase food security, and mitigate climate change." They do so much life-changing work!
  https://awellfedworld.org

- **Milk Hurts & Mothers Against Dairy**: Both projects expose the horrors of the dairy industry and the deadly impact it has on our bodies, the earth, and the nonhuman victims of the industry themselves. Mothers Against Dairy shares real stories from human mothers that connect and relate to mothers of the dairy industry.
  MH: *https://www.facebook.com/MilkHurts*
  MAD: *https://mothersagainstdairy.org*

- **Switch4Good**: I can't even put into words how helpful this organization is in helping people eliminate animal-based dairy from their lives. They host an informative podcast, are animal and human rights activists, and are fighting against dietary racism.

https://switch4good.org

- **9 Steps for Easy Vegan Travel** by Wendy Werneth & Happy Cow: This free download is great for beginner vegans who are ready to travel or long-time veg heads who are traveling for the first time and nervous about finding plant-based food!
https://www.happycow.net/moozine/steps-to-be-vegan

6

How to Network and Find Work

"Traveling is a brutality. It forces you to trust strangers and to lose sight of all that familiar comfort of home and friends. You are constantly off balance. Nothing is yours except the essential things – air, sleep, dreams, the sea, the sky – all things tending towards the eternal or what we imagine of it."

- Cesare Pavese

How To Network and Find Work

Focus on multiplying your energies without having to do the labor each time!

1. Networking

In this section, we'll go over a few of the most important things you need to know about networking. If you master one thing in your travels, consider mastering this:

What do I mean by networking?

When I talk about networking here, I mean creating connections with others, even if you don't know them. And then letting them create more connections for you.

Why would I want to network? Networking is important. Every time you create a new connection, you've possibly stored some energy to use later in the universe. For example, if you're looking for a place to stay in Alabama, you may post a status on Facebook stating your request. Because you've already networked and have made friends while traveling who can see your status, they may be able to help you fulfill your needs by finding you a place to stay. In this case, you didn't have to do much work.

You didn't have to run around Alabama, knocking on doors, in search of a couch. You didn't have to message a handful of people on Couchsurfing asking for a place to stay. All you had to do was state your need and let others do the work of finding a way to fulfill it. You did the work up front by staying in touch with people you've met during previous travels.

You can use networking to find jobs, places to stay, transportation, and potential travel partners without approaching each one individually.

How do I network?

The task itself isn't as hard as it seems. As you travel and move through life, keep a mental or physical file on who you meet and what they possibly have to offer. The cool thing is we really don't know folks as well as we think we do! They can be of big, and unexpected, help.

Facebook is a great place to network. Whenever I am searching for jobs, places to stay, care, or transportation in a specific area, I make a post on Facebook. My Facebook connections are then able to offer me what they have or find someone else (that I usually don't know) who is able to help.

Hot Tip: When you meet people during travels, try to stay connected with them in some way. That doesn't mean you have to talk to them every day, or even every few months, but you have some access to them if needed, and them to you. I like to add people on Facebook, Instagram, and even get their phone numbers, email and mailing address. Everyone loves getting snail mail, and what better way to stay in touch or brighten someone's day!

Everyday interactions are opportunities to network as well. You know the person you chatted with at the coffee shop? They may have a friend able to take you to your next destination. Remember the person you met at a poetry slam? They may be able to hook you up with a job at that local coffee shop.

My point is, folks...the world can work in some wonderful ways if you set it up and give it time. Some of my favorite memories, people that I've spent time with, and travel partners have come through for me by the recommendation of others. Although it seems like we're touching on ways to get your needs met here, keep in mind it's just as important for you to give back, how and where you can, when you're ready and able.

Food for the Brain

On one of my last trips in the USA, I felt some travel magic playing out while I was in New Mexico. About a month before, I was at an animal rights conference in California. While I was there, I connected with another activist from North Carolina. We discussed my travel plans, and I mentioned I was looking for work in the near future. A couple weeks after we parted, the same person messaged me telling me they had found possible work for me. They had a friend who lived in New Mexico (one of the states on my list) who needed help for about a month at their home. After talking more and working out the details, we were able to set something up. When I got to New Mexico, I spent a month with them working constantly and getting to know the family.

After the month was up, I got paid. This then allowed me to travel, without working, for a full month after leaving New Mexico. I used the cash I earned to take buses, rent a car to explore the Grand Tetons and Yellowstone National Park, and enjoy some tasty food. My friend Sara and I didn't have to worry about working as we went because we were already set.

During the same stay in New Mexico, I was posting pictures and updates to my friends on Facebook. One of them suggested I meet up with their friends who lived in a town I planned on exploring. I chatted with the friends of a friend and set up a time to meet them. When I got to Taos, we met at a restaurant and talked over plant-based tacos. I only planned to stay for a short amount of time because I wanted to drive back to Santa Fe before it got dark. I ended up really digging their energy and we talked for a couple hours. It was refreshing to meet such energetic and inspirational people and to open up about things that had been weighing heavy on my mind. I couldn't have appreciated their presence more and what they gave me that night. I ended up coming back twice to stay in the tiny home of one of the women I met named Angie! If you're ready to learn about how to reduce waste, live more consciously, get direct alternative living tips, Angie really brings it. You can find the podcast episode we recorded together in the resources at the end of this chapter.

2. How to Find Work

Simmer down folks, because this is an important section. People often approach me feeling lost when it comes to finding work on the road. The more you network, the easier it is. I repeat: *The more you network, the easier it is!*

On my first trip across the USA, I was constantly working. I started that trip with a few hundred dollars and used the money I did have to repair my bike. So, every time I needed food, I found work. Every time I needed extra cash to buy a bus ticket, I found work.

Because I was working so much, I was networking and making connections left and right. On some occasions, I would walk into a restaurant, asking to work for a meal, and walk out with various odd jobs, a place to stay, and a steady supply of food. While I completed these tasks, I got to spend time with new people, explore new places, and walk away with cash in my pocket.

How can I find work in the first place?

Finding work while traveling is not as complicated as you may think. Many factors and privileges can play into this experience as well.

Where should I be looking for work?

Look everywhere—up, down, and all around. Some examples of places to ask are small local businesses, restaurants, hostels, cafes, and any other shops or stores you see in town. If you know of a local farmer who doesn't actively exploit animals (they only work with vegetables and other plants), that may be a good place to check as well.

What do I say?

When you find a place you'd like to ask for work at, it's simple. Walk in and ask for what you need. Use the same model we did in **chapter six**, but tailor the introduction to meet your current work needs. After you do it a couple times you may start to feel more at ease and confidence in your own ability to ask for what you need.

Food for the Brain

On my bike tour across the USA, I found myself in a little town, searching for work, so I could leave the same town. This is where I walked into a restaurant looking for food and walked out with a job and a place to stay.

Before I hit the jackpot, I was wandering around downtown, wanting to make some cash. I saw a small, local business that sold furniture. When I walked in I learned that the person behind the counter was the owner. After introducing myself, and stating my needs, they immediately put me to work vacuuming the floor. When I was done with that task, I picked up some rags and spray and began to wipe everything down. After about an hour and a half, the job was done. I left a spotless store with cash in hand.

I then strolled over to a restaurant nearby and asked the hostess if I could work for a meal. She turned me down quickly, but I saw a sparkle of thoughtfulness cross her face. She told me that her brother was a single dad and needed help taking care of his kid and cleaning the house while he worked because his helper was out of town. Jackpot! The next day her brother picked me up from the park that I was sleeping at and took me to his house. For around four days I acted as a babysitter, cleaner, and houseguest. I had landed a safe place to sleep, fresh food (that was left over from the restaurant that I was originally trying to find work at), companionship, and a way to make money.

On my bike touring trip, I had an easier time finding work because of all of the networking I did the year before, and all of the connections I kept up with. During the bike tour, I ended up alone, cold, frustrated, and crying, standing in someone's driveway. I didn't know it was a driveway... until they tried to pull in, which required me to move my tired and crying body out of the way.

To make a long story short, this couple took me in, treated me like their own child, and endlessly showed me care and affection. I ended up working with them on their catering company crew, learning a new skill, and attending a couple of events.

A couple of years later, when I was back in California, they already had a job lined up for me. I spent four days with them, working hard, and came out with $400. That, to me, is incredibly useful when traveling. If I hadn't been searching for work or networking so much on my first trip, I would have had to spend more time searching for work on that specific trip.

Consider WWOOFing

No, I don't mean barking like a dog. WWOOF (Worldwide Opportunities on Organic Farms) USA is an online space where you can connect with organic farms all across the USA (also available in other countries), and work for them. While WWOOFing, you usually work at least five half days, around 4-5 hours a day, in exchange for food and a place to stay.

To use WWOOF you have to be 18 years old or older and pay a yearly membership that costs $40 in the USA. (12) To learn about WWOOF opportunities in other countries you'll have to visit the country-specific site. You are also provided a wide variety of options on your length of stay. You can choose anywhere from one day, multiple weeks, months, or long term.

On the WWOOF website, they call themselves an "educational and cultural exchange program." (13) I have found this to be true; every time I have WWOOFed, no matter what kind of taste the experience left in my mouth, I've learned something. While WWOOFing, you're likely to meet other travelers and folks from other countries.

- To sign up, head over to **wwoofusa.org**. Once there, you'll be able to find more information or sign up for a membership to get started.

- Click "SIGN UP" in the top right-hand corner of the page. Then click on "WWOOFER MEMBERSHIP."

- From here, you'll be taken to another page which asks questions about safety and security.

- Next, you'll be prompted to add your personal information. Enter your new username, password, name, and address.

- Click "NEXT," and it'll take you to the payment page. You'll be required to enter your name and credit card information.

- After everything is set up and processed, you're in! The next big step is creating a profile that host farms will be able to see.

- Make sure to fill this section out honestly and thoroughly. If you need some guidance as to how to answer bio questions, refer back to the assistance that I offered in the Couchsurfing section of this guide.

When you're ready to start WWOOFing, the process is fairly simple.

- Log in to the website. Click "FIND A FARM." From here, you'll be able to modify your search. I suggest doing this: Enter the state or zip code that you'll be in, length of stay, and I always click on "Vegan Friendly" under the "FARM TYPE" option. Once you have all of your information entered, click on "APPLY FILTERS."

- The farms that meet your needs will show up on the map to the right. Zoom in to take a better look at their locations. Click on the dots that represent farms to find out more about each specific farm.

- Once on a farm profile, you'll be able to read more about it, check out their reviews, and contact them if you're interested.

- After you've decided that you want to WWOOF on a specific farm, click the contact button on their profile. A large number of farms also include other contact routes, such as their email or a phone number. Calling someone is the quickest and most direct way to begin your WWOOFing process.

- From here, farms will most likely want to spend some time asking you more questions. They're looking to see if you are a good fit for their farm. Express your needs, wants, and expectations directly!

Once you've landed a farming gig, all you have to do is show up. Each farm is different so when you're talking to the owners make sure to ask detailed questions and gather all of the information that you're looking for. They may think you're a good fit for the farm, but the farm may not be a good fit for you. Ask, ask, ask! Leave no stone unturned.

Hot Tip: Instead of officially WWOOFing, why not try to connect with a vegan animal sanctuary? They provide refuge and forever homes for neglected, abused, unwanted, exploited, and sick nonhuman animals. Often these individuals come from or escape the deathly clutches of animal agriculture. Please be mindful that not every vegan animal sanctuary is open to visitors or work exchangers, though. Some sanctuary founders and animal caregivers are overworked and stretched thin. Sometimes having outsiders or inexperienced volunteers can create extra work. With that being said, other sanctuaries have specific programs set up for work exchanges or internships, and love to have new helpers and volunteers. While working at a sanctuary, you can expect to work with all types of amazing people such as ducks, cows, chickens, roosters, turkeys, horses, pigs, goats, sheep, llamas, alpacas, rabbits, geese, fish, and more.

Your duties may include helping with feeding shifts, scooping poop, managing pastures, administering medication, and giving an abundance of appreciated belly-rubs and cow kisses. You can find a list of sanctuaries across the USA in the resources below. It never hurts to reach out to ones you are interested in and write to them to ask if they do work exchanges!

I will also list some of my favorite vegan sanctuaries that aren't open for work exchanges but love giving tours and having volunteers at the end of the book. Spending time with farmed animals in a loving, safe, and supportive environment is such a special experience. With the right setting their personalities and quirks are easily able to shine through. Have you ever spent your afternoon lounging with cows or giving a demanding pig an hour-long belly rub? If not, you are missing out!

If you can, consider donating to any sanctuary you tour. Even the smallest chunk of change goes a long way in a sanctuary! If you aren't able to connect with any vegan sanctuaries in person, connect with them online and step into a whole new world of compassion, love, acceptance, joy, and care. Follow sanctuaries on social media and share! This is a simple, free, and effective form of activism.

Food for the Brain

Thus far in my traveling career, I've WWOOFed a handful of times. Each place I stayed was *extremely* different. The first time I experienced WWOOFing was on a small goat farm in Virginia, right before I started my bike tour. Some of my duties included feeding the animals, cleaning stalls, painting the barn, and cleaning out the water tubs. Because I live vegan, I decided I wouldn't milk the goats, collect eggs, make soap that had stolen goat milk in it, or anything else that didn't align with my values. This was an important conversation for us to have before I stepped foot onto the farm (I now wouldn't WOOF on a farm that exploits/uses animals).

The owners of the farm were interesting. Although we were very different, we enjoyed our time together and really brought some new energies into each other's lives. During my stay at this farm, the owner's brother passed away. She had to go to New York to take care of things, leaving me and her partner at the farm. Her partner worked on a military base and was gone most of the day.

I quickly learned how to do all of the tasks that needed to be completed. Soon, I was running the farm. The one thing that I valued the most was spending time with the other animals—goats, chickens, ducks, dogs, cats, pigs, and a llama—that lived on the farm. There was one person who captured my heart more than anyone: Bertie the pig.

Not all WWOOFing experiences have such happy endings, though. During the summer of 2017 I WWOOFed on a farm in Los Angeles. When I talked to the owner she assured me I would be a great fit for the farm. Looking at the profile, pictures, and information, I agreed with her.

Soon after arriving at the farm, I realized it was lacking some important elements such as funds and organization. The absence of solid direction and clarity from the owner complicated the process of making any real progress on tasks. We would all finish one job that we had spent hours on, and she would come through and tell us to completely change it. Although she had

seemingly good intentions, working on that farm really tried my patience. She also lacked the sufficient funds to feed everyone at the time, so we would buy food and then give them our receipts, to get paid back sometime in the future. At one point, a few of us got sent out to the desert of Palmdale. We were staying in an abandoned house that had no electricity, security, water, or cooling system. It was hot and brutal. Temperatures would easily pass 100 degrees and we would all be fighting to not overheat. The house didn't feel secure, and when we were cleaning it out before our stay, we found lots of needles and other items that were being used for drugs. It wasn't an ideal situation.

My expectations of what would happen on the farm, and in the desert, were not met. There was a lot of drama, crying, confusion, and arguing at the farm. On the flip side, I met the most amazing group of humans there who happened to be WWOOFing at the same time as me. We were quite a diverse group, and we quickly and solidly bonded. Through all of the challenges that I experienced on that farm, leaving them was the hardest.

Consider Workaway

A program exists that is very similar to WWOOFing, and it's called Workaway. For Workaway, you exchange a few hours of volunteering per day for food and board. The only difference is the jobs include much more variety! You could find yourself doing housework, manual labor projects, cooking, childcare, animal care, teaching, or helping at hotels and hostels. There are jobs that can be done to meet the host's specific needs, but make sure to find a job that meets yours, too.

As of 2021, Workaway is $44.00 a year for a single person and $56.00 to sign up as a couple or as two friends, no matter how many times you use it. (14) For more information, go to **workaway.info**, where they provide videos, photos, and blogs to help you better understand what your exchange might be like.

Safety tips for networking and looking for work:
- Be alert and aware when meeting new people. Just because someone you know recommended an activity, person, or place to you doesn't mean it's the best option.
- Trust your feelings and walk-through new situations with care.
- Don't give out your exact locations, or plans, on social media. It's okay to post about a larger idea, or general place, but you never can be 100% sure what people will do with your information.

Mantras:
- Travel magic is constantly working in my favor, bringing me the right people, situations, ideas, and solutions.
- I am confident that the universe has received my requests, and that it is already lining them up for me.

Resources:
- ***How To Travel on A Tight Budget - A Complete Guide to Begin Now:*** This resource is one of the first articles that I published on my blog. It is basically a summary of this book, but in article form. It's helpful to have it saved while traveling, or to share with others, as a quick reminder of this information.

http://wanderwoman.online/index.php/2017/05/07/travel-with-no-money/

- ***How To Travel the USA for Free (Without Mooching):*** This article is great and super helpful—it's the first thing that I truly investigated when I was beginning to plan and form my own ideas around traveling with almost no money. Rob talks about a few things that I don't cover and has a different story. Our experiences are different because of how we present, our contrasting privileges, and who we are. http://robgreenfield.tv/travel-america-for-free/
- ***Farm Animal Sanctuary Directory: Visit Shelters Worldwide:*** Explore a list of vegan animal sanctuaries across the USA. *https://vegan.com/blog/sanctuaries/*
- **The Sanctuary Tour Podcast:** Visit sanctuaries across the country with me as your host! Learn why sanctuaries start, how they operate, and what their missions are. Hear the stories of their resilient residents. *http://sanctuarytour.org*

7

What To Bring

"There are people
who put their dreams in a little box
and say, 'Yes, I've got dreams,
of course I've got dreams.'
Then they put the box away
and bring it out once in a while to look in it,
and yep, they're still there."

- Emma Bombeck

What to Bring

Now you've made it through the bulk of the book, let's talk about some physical tools that will help support you while living out these experiences along the way. I'm about to share my personal packing list with you. Try not to feel overwhelmed if you don't have these things. We can find them and it doesn't have to cost you an arm and a leg. Your own list will look a little different depending on who you are and where you are going!

Where can I find needed travel items and gear?

When looking for travel gear I encourage you to buy used. You can find fully functional items for the least amount of dollars or possibly for free. Check out web spaces like **Craigslist, Facebook Yard Sales,** and **eBay.** Consider asking the folks around you if they have anything they'd like to offer that's still hanging around on your list. Check out your local used adventure shops. Consignment shops and Goodwill stores also have awesome used items. If you decide to buy items, use the information we went over in **chapter two**, about how to make

extra cash before you go.

Here's my go-to list for solo backpacking:

- **One-person tent**
- **Sleeping bag**
- **Blanket**

- **Cellphone**
- **GPS**
- **Needed maps**
- **SPOT tracker device**
- **Charger for electronics**
- **Solar-powered charger**
- **Power bank (external battery)**
- **Headphones**

- **Mace**
- **Taser**
- **Whistle**
- **Flashlight**
- **ID**
- **Journal**
- **Writing tool**
- **Written emergency contact list**

- **First aid kit**
- **Bug spray**
- **Lotion**
- **Sunblock** – Please try to get one safe for rivers, oceans, and streams! I will share an article below in the resources why this is important and what brands you can look for.
- **Soap/shampoo/conditioner** – Again, get something safe for rivers, oceans, and streams.

You can find a version of each of these items listed below that don't contain animal products.

- **Spoon and fork** – See if you can find bamboo sets to buy locally! If not, To-Go Ware sells them at outfitter stores or online.
- **Water bottle or water bladder and cup for coffee or tea**
- **Zip lock bags**
- **Cooking gear** – Camp stove and propane
- **Pot or pan**

- **Weather-appropriate clothing** – Not necessarily what's most expensive, but whatever fits the needs of your specific trip.

- **Jacket or coat**
- **Shoes and socks**
- **Hiking boots**
- **Sunglasses**
- **Swimsuit**

- **Any other desired items** - This may include vitamins, pills, supplements, or anything else necessary to your well-being.

- **Menstrual cup**
- **Panty liners**
- **Period undies** – Learn more about this magical invention in the resources below!

Extras:
- **Books**
- **Yoga mat**
- **Phone case**
- **Snacks**
- **Computer**
- **Camera**

Pack it up! After you have all of your items collected and together, it's time to pack them up. What type of luggage will you be using? I recommend using a backpack every time. It offers a sufficient amount of space, external straps to attach more things, and possibly an easier and more mobile way to carry your items with you.

Resources:

- ***Traveling Thailand: Don't Make My Big Mistakes****:* Read the article that I wrote after learning how to be more ocean and earth-friendly with the products that I bought and used while spending a month in Thailand. *http://wanderwoman.online/index.php/2019/09/10/thailand-mistakes/*

- **Thinx Period Undies**: I used to use regular tampons but did not like the constant cost and waste. I then switched to the diva cup, which I still sometimes use, but often while traveling I need something more versatile, comfy, and stronger to compliment my cycle. Period undies are like normal underwear but with a built-in leak-proof pad. They come in all different styles and levels of protection. Learn more about them, why I use them, and get $10 off when shopping through my link! *https://shethinx.com/unruly*

8

When You Return

"Whoever you are,
or whatever it is that you do,
when you really want something,
it's because that desire originated
in the soul of the universe.
It's your mission on earth."

-Paulo Coelho

When You Return

As you can see, we've skipped from what to pack to when you return. What happens in the middle is entirely up to you. I have to say, reader, I have so much love for you and your desire for adventure. I can feel it and hope you can feel it too. I'm here to offer support and I wouldn't be doing so if I didn't present this discussion of what happens when you return.

If you've traveled before you may already understand what I'm talking about here. Every time you leave and return, you have undeniably made some changes in your life or in yourself. For me, I've found coming back, or pausing my travels, can be one of the hardest parts of the process. After five months on the road I'm usually pretty excited about dreaming and snoozing in my own bed, seeing familiar faces, and revisiting some old habits. But these things don't cover up the pain I often feel when my travel experiences come to a close.

Like I said before, this type of travel doesn't have to be temporary, it can be a lifestyle. I now understand and fully believe that. There are a few things that are helpful for me to think about and start to process before closing the book on a trip.

You May Change While Others Stay the Same

I feel when you're moving through the world experiencing travel, you often learn, grow, and change more quickly. You are constantly exposed to new people, places, and ideas. *So how could you not?* Each time I finish a trip, I notice I'm forever changed. I often feel frustrated when I return to my "stable" setting to find others aren't too different. Sure, they are learning and changing too, every day. But to me the growth isn't always comparable or as fast. Consider this before the end of your trip. If you don't, you may find yourself feeling more surprised and frustrated than you thought you would.

"How was your trip?"

People love to ask this question. And to this, I say, *I can't really say*. I can give people a general overview of places I went, events I attended, and activities I did, but it's hard to put the rest into words. With one simple question, someone is asking you to quickly sum up your total experience, and this may seem hard to do—or even be annoying at times. And that's okay. Nine out of ten times, people are genuinely interested in your experience. I like to return the intention back to them by explaining exactly what I know: that I'm still processing my experiences, and it is hard to quickly summarize. For me personally, I'm usually excited to share about my trip: what I did that made everything new, who I met that inspired and touched me, and how I intentionally crafted my experiences. So, if someone is truly interested, I like to take a little bit more time and space to explore that with them.

How to Mentally Transition

I'm a very in-my-body-when-I'm-in-my-body type of person. So physically, I like to use items and the physical space around me to transition from a trip and back into my space. This may not resonate with everyone. It's just something I've found that helps me personally. When I start to settle, I take my time unpacking my bag. Each day I remove the items I need and unpack little by little. When I've unloaded and dumped everything out at once in the past, it has felt too sharp.

I often wear only the clothes I was traveling with for a couple weeks. For me, when I arrive back to some sort of "home space" from a trip, I have way more clothing options than what I carried with me. During my trips, my clothes often become more meaningful to me: things that keep me warm, safe, and let me express myself. When I return, I often feel overwhelmed with the choices and lack of connection to my other items. Wearing the same travel clothes I've been with until I feel like moving out of that space feels supportive to me.

The last thing I do to mentally transition is sleep on my own couch or someplace other than my bed. It creates the feeling that I'm still on the go and not quite settled into a set structure. As silly as it sounds, this is the most helpful physical action for me. Journaling is also a great way to process your memories and feelings!

Now that you're back, you may notice some questions and feelings come up. Some of the first ones I would get hung up on, and that felt the largest to me, have always been, "Is my trip really over? Is this it?" The answer: it doesn't have to be.

Just as you've crafted your travel experiences, you can craft your life in a similar way. The new people, places, and experiences introduced into your life will always be a part of you, and you get the pleasure of keeping those memories stored during the rest of your time on Earth. Let them mold you, inspire you, change your habits, and breathe new breath into your life. Now that you've seen more of the world, you will never fit back into your old molds again.

Can you see how magical that is?

Dear readers,

I want to close this book by sending my gratitude straight to you. All of you have supported me on my travels, spilling into my life in some way.

Some of you have shared meals with me, taken me on unforgettable adventures, introduced me to your hometowns, and let me step into your lives without hesitation. All of you have opened your hearts to me. By reading this guide, you've allowed me to be a part of your experience going forth, and I can't find the words to tell you how thankful I am for that.

Please remember I am available to you. If you have any specific questions, need another brain to help find a solution, or are looking for connections, I'm your person. My support doesn't stop on the last page of this book.

My wish for you is that as you travel, you learn how to craft your experiences, and feel that travel magic. I hope you learn how to receive fully and give just as much. It's because of people like you I can experience my travels in such an unconventional and fulfilling way, and we can learn to support each other on this wild journey.

From a heart bursting with love,
Calen Ann Otto

The Author:

Calen Ann Otto is a travel blogger, activist, writer, and podcaster who often settles near Asheville, North Carolina. They identify as queer and vegan, and they let these experiences come through and craft their work in many ways.

"Home" for Calen is where their parents, partner, closest humans, and animal companions are. Calen finds home in their yoga practice and in the authenticity of others. When they are not writing they can often be found jumping in the closest body of cold water, initiating an ecstatic dance party, or laying in the dirt, soaking in the rays of the sun.

Calen has traveled across the USA multiple times and has been to five continents. They plan on continuing to expand their travels and sharing their findings, stories, and travel knowledge with readers everywhere!

The Editors:

Charlie Sudlow-Maestas is a queer, trans nonbinary, polyamorous artist living in Albuquerque, New Mexico. They live with two cats, three rats, and two dogs. All of the humans and dogs living in the house are ethical vegans. Charlie is passionate about intersectional feminism, disability justice, and all things sex, sexuality, and gender-related. In their free time, Charlie enjoys reading, making art, and talking with their best friend soulmate, Calen (the amazing author of this guide).

Charlie is currently finishing their two Bachelor of Arts degrees in Women, Gender, and Sexuality Studies and Sociology at the University of New Mexico. They plan to continue their education through graduate school and would love to become a sex educator.

Find Charlie on Instagram:
https://www.instagram.com/charlietherainbowunicorn/

Listen to Calen & Charlie's podcast episode:
https://soundcloud.com/unrulystories/pleasure-in-a-pandemic-how-to-solo-or-with-a-partner

Helen Otto is a mom, wife, activist, leader, and elementary principal. She enjoys reading, camping, spending time in nature and at the beach. Additionally, Helen has an interest in making homemade soap and shampoos in order to promote self-care without plastic. Her vegan lifestyle reflects her love of feeling healthy, animals, and the earth.

Kim Beller, a North Carolina mixed media artist, lives with her family and rescued animals in the Blue Ridge Mountains just outside of Asheville. In addition to art, Kim is a passionate humane educator and vegan, an avid reader, a waterfall chaser, and nature lover. One of her favorite things to do is visit sanctuaries and play her harmonium for the rescued animals.

Kim's passion for reading books, (sometimes multiple books at a time) opened the door to her editing books and articles. Always up for a good vegan friendly travel guide, Kim was honored to help with the editing of *The Art of Unruly Travel on a Budget*!

Kim is the host of a vegan Airbnb cottage in the Blue Ridge Mountains and loves meeting new visitors. She teaches art classes and workshops specializing in art journaling, intuitive painting, book making, vegan cooking, and more.

Find Kim's art: *kimbellerart.com*
Listen to Kim's podcast: *https://soundcloud.com/artnestpodcast*

Tim Burdine is a natural builder who lives off-grid in the mountains of North Carolina. He is also an avid gardener and sells his veganic produce at the farmers markets on a sliding scale. When Tim is not gardening, you can usually find him hiking the A.T., reading books on natural building, modifying his cob home, chasing waterfalls, or thinking about his next project. Tim believes in sustainability, veganism, and simple living.

Christy Morgan has been tantalizing taste buds for over 15 years as a vegan chef, cooking instructor, food writer, and cookbook author. Her mission is to show that a vegan diet and lifestyle can be delicious & easy, will bring more energy and bliss into your life all while helping the animals and the planet. Christy became obsessed with fitness post-30 and is a NASM certified personal trainer and yoga teacher spreading the message that you can be strong & thrive on a vegan diet. She can show you how to reach all your health and fitness goals to reach optimal health. Having visited over 51 countries she loves sharing her passions of travel with others with wellness retreats all over the world!

Visit her website: *blissfulandfit.com*

105 Publishing is a 100% Black owned publishing company that brings author's books to life without any hidden agendas. Founder, J.L. Raynor, and co-owner, Patricia Jones, work together helping individuals through the self-publishing process by offering many services. Their motto is "We Will Exceed Your Expectations!"

Join the Unruly Travel Network:

https://www.facebook.com/groups/unrulytravellers

Find more of
Calen's work:

Instagram: @unruly_traveller
Facebook: @Unruly Travel
TikTok: @unruly_traveller

Blog: *unrulytravel.com*

Podcast: *https://soundcloud.com/unrulystories*

The Unruly Podcast can also be found on Apple Podcasts, Spotify, and wherever you stream podcasts!

Vlog:
https://www.youtube.com/channel/UCFEljaVxBODs9wlFUGh QVFws

Included Websites:

2. Preparing to Leave
- gofundme.com
- facebook.com
- craigslist.com
- ebay.com

3. How to Get Around
- *https://en.wikipedia.org/wiki/List of people who have walked across the United States)*
- adventurecycling.com
- youtube.com
- warmshowers.com
- google.com
- amtrack.com
- momondo.com
- wanderu.com
- greyhound.com
- megabus.com
- cheapoair.com
- cheapflights.com
- freecampsites.net

4. Where to Stay
- couchsurfing.com
- airbnb.com
- hostelworld.com
- freecampsites.net
- blm.gov
- park4night.com

5. How to Find Food
- *http://robgreenfield.tv/arrestedfordumpsterdiving/*
- wwoofusa.org

6. How To Find Work and Network
- workaway.info

- wwoofusa.org

Mental/Emotional Support Hotlines

Depression And Suicide:
- National Suicide Prevention Hotline: 1-800-273-8255
- The Trevor Project: 866-488-7386:

Eating Disorders:

- National Eating Disorder Association: 1-800-931-2237

General Crisis:

- Crisis Text Line: Text SUPPORT to 741-741

Sexual Assault:
- Rape, Abuse and Incest National Network: 1-800-656-4673:

  Offers 24/7 help

Queer Centered:

- The Gay, Lesbian, Bisexual and Transgender National Hotline:

  888-843-4564

- The GLBT National Youth Talkline (Youth serving youth through

  age 25): 800- 246-7743

- Trans Lifeline: 877- 565-8860

- The National Runaway Safeline: 800-RUNAWAY (800-786-2929)

- The True Colors United: 212-461-4401

More Support and Resources

7 Hotlines That Exist in Case You Need Them:
https://spoonuniversity.com/healthier/7-hotlines-that-exist-in-case-you-need-them

Support Hotlines (Queer Centered): _https://pflag.org/hotlines_

55 Mental Health Resources for People of Color:
https://www.onlinemswprograms.com/resources/social-issues/mental-health-resources-racial-ethnic-groups/

LGBTQIA Resource Center: _https://lgbtqia.ucdavis.edu/support/hotlines_

Suggested Sanctuaries:

4Them Sanctuary, TN: *https://4themsanctuary.org*

Barn Sanctuary, MI: *https://www.barnsanctuary.org*

Cotton Branch, SC: *https://www.cottonbranch.org*

Farm Sanctuary: *https://www.farmsanctuary.org*

NM Farm Sanctuary, NM:
https://www.facebook.com/nmfarmsanctuary/

Rowdy Girl Sanctuary, TX: *https://rowdygirlsanctuary.org*

Sanctuary Moon, MI: *https://www.facebook.com/SanctuaryMoon.org/*

SiSu Refuge, NC: *https://sisurefuge.org*

Sweet Olive Farm, GA: *https://sweetolivefarm.org*

Ziggy's Refuge Farm Sanctuary, NC:
https://www.facebook.com/ZiggysRefuge/

Sources:

(1) Quocle, B. (2018). How to Walk Across America: 22 Steps (with pictures). Accessed April 16 2021 through *https://www.instructables.com/EXTREME-Walking-How-To-Walk-Across-America/*

(2) Baumer, M. (2010). I am a Road. Accessed March 4 2017 through *https://thebaumer.com/iamaroad*

(3) Amtrak. Making Reservations for Passengers with a Disability. Accessed April 16, 2021, through *https://www.amtrak.com/planning-booking/accessible-travel-services/making-reservations-for-passengers-with-a-disability.html*

(4) Amtrak. Carry-On Baggage. Accessed April 16, 2021, through *https://www.amtrak.com/carry-on-baggage*

(5) Amtrak. At the Station. Accessed April 16, 2021, through *https://www.amtrak.com/at-the-station.html*

(6) Greyhound. Ticket Info. Accessed April 16, 2021, through *https://www.greyhound.com/en/help-and-info/ticket-info*

(7) Megabus. Luggage Policy. Accessed April 16, 2021, through *https://us.megabus.com/luggage-policy*

(8) Bike PGH. (2011). Anyone Taken A Bike On Megabus? | Message Board. Accessed April 16, 2021, through *https://bikepgh.org/message-board/topic/anyone-taken-a-bike-on-megabus/*

(9) Couchsurfing Blog. (2020). We hear you. Accessed April 16, 2021, through *https://blog.couchsurfing.com/we-hear-you/*

(10) U.S. Department of the Interior Bureau of Land Management. Official Website. Accessed April 16, 2021, through *https://www.blm.gov/*

(11) Greenfield, R. (2015). Arrested for dumpster diving for food? I've got you covered. Accessed April 16, 2021, through *https://www.robgreenfield.org/arrestedfordumpsterdiving/*

(12) WWOOF USA. How It Works. Accessed April 16, 2021, through https://wwoofusa.org/how-it-works/basics